What Your Colleagues Are Saying . . .

"This book is packed with useful ideas, strategies, and clear action steps for supporting new teacher induction with a student-centered philosophy at its core. In both translating the research and describing educators' lived experiences, Amanda Brueggeman has created a timely resource that will resonate with classroom teachers, school and district leaders. When put into practice, the strategies in this book will help in shaping mastery environments in which everyone in an educational setting shares the belief that individually and collectively they have the capability to impact positive improvement."

—Jenni Donohoo
Provincial Literacy Lead Council of Ontario Directors of Education
Author, *Collective Efficacy*

"*Student-Centered Mentoring: Keeping Students at the Heart of New Teachers' Learning* is a thoughtful and timely book. Amanda Brueggeman's core belief that 'empowering others to grow and make an impact on students is important for our future' gets at both a practical and moral imperative: we need ways of supporting new teachers that are compassionate and impactful if we want to change the trajectory of the teacher shortage we currently face. With practical tips, a solid framework, and plenty of examples from her own experience in the field, *Student-Centered Mentoring* does just that."

—Leanna Harris
Author and Consultant, Diane Sweeney Consulting

"*Student-Centered Mentoring: Keeping Students at the Heart of New Teachers' Learning* is a welcomed resource in an untapped market. Amanda Brueggeman's book provides specific student-centered strategies, tips, and tools for mentors to utilize while partnering with new teachers to propel student learning. By putting students at the heart of mentoring, new teachers will be provided with ongoing and meaningful support that allows them to reflect and refine instruction based on current student evidence. This is a must read for anyone who supports new teachers, mentors, coaches, principals, and district leadership."

—Joy Casey
Consultant, Diane Sweeney Consulting

"Given the complexity of the teaching profession, individuals beginning their career need comprehensive support with systems, pedagogy, and meeting students' needs while managing their own. There are many approaches districts take to equip these ambitious colleagues. *Student-Centered Mentoring: Keeping Students at the Heart of New Teachers' Learning* creates a unique layered process for developing the mentor's skillset to meet the teachers' learning needs while establishing the student focus from day one. Undoubtedly, Amanda Brueggeman's system, including the strategies and action steps provided, will transform the impact mentors have on our newest colleagues as well as the students they serve well beyond their first years."

—Julie Steele
Consultant, Diane Sweeney Consulting

"*Student-Centered Mentoring* is an inspiring guide for any educator tasked with supporting new teachers. We all know that being a new teacher involves a unique set of challenges. This book presents a multilayered approach to support the varied needs of new teachers, all while keeping student engagement and growth at the center of mentor-mentee's collective work. Full of questions mentors can ask new teachers to support effective management and instruction, processes for goal-setting and reflecting, and tips for giving effective feedback, this resource allows us to envision the power of collaborative partnerships to build new teacher confidence and give the essential support that is often lacking in induction programs today."

—Amber Birch Trujillo
Consultant, Diane Sweeney Consulting

"As we think about teaching and learning in the era of Covid-19, *Student-Centered Mentoring: Keeping Students at the Heart of New Teachers' Learning* is essential. Now more than ever, we have a collective imperative to develop beliefs and habits of mind in new teachers that serve students in meaningful, enduring ways. Bringing together the latest research on teacher development, trends in teaching and learning, and a robust set of anecdotes, Amanda Brueggeman does a masterful job at laying a foundation for those in charge of new teacher development programs. The way that she advocates for student-centered mentoring will help new and veteran teachers alike remain energized by the work we're all called to do as educators."

—Quinton P. Walker
Head of the High School
University School of Nashville, TN

"*Student-Centered Mentoring* is a must-read for every mentor, instructional coach, and educational leader. Amanda Brueggeman's book shares the limitless possibilities of fostering relationships, building engaging dynamics, and creating effective change through mentorships! Her work is both student-centered and teacher-supportive. She illuminates the possibilities of building teacher leadership and fostering teacher capacity. She offers strategies on collaboration, navigating difficult dialogue, and grounding this work in keeping our students at the focus. This book is an educator's dream!"

—Jigisha Vyas
Instructional Coach
Wyckoff School District, NJ

"In the ever-evolving field of education, it is critical for new teachers to begin their careers with the ongoing support and guidance of a mentor. *Student-Centered Mentoring* offers precise, practical strategies for mentors to help mentees establish systems of beliefs and practices that keep student learning at the forefront of teaching. Envisioning "school as a system with student growth at the heart," this resource provides readers with recommendations for examining philosophies, scenarios to guide learning, and frameworks to create a deep and sustainable system of mentorship. The wide range of joys and challenges experienced when mentoring new teachers is presented with the ultimate (and attainable) goal of improving outcomes for all students."

—Sarah Valter
Literacy Coach
Lindbergh Schools, MO

"This book is a must-have for mentors. Amanda Brueggeman advocates for a shift from a traditional, top-down mentoring model, where new teacher and mentor conversations revolve around the most important reason for teaching: students. The author explains how mentors can build the capacity of new teachers through reflective conversations about their existing skills, mindsets, and how to understand and assess the effect their teaching moves have on student learning outcomes. The strategies and action steps presented in each chapter provide mentors with a variety of methods to engage their new teacher, from emotional intelligence to collaborative learning experiences."

—Rachel Jenner
Instructional Coach/Consultant
Rockingham County Public Schools, VA

"*Student-Centered Mentoring: Keeping Students at the Heart of New Teacher's Learning* is a must read for anyone who is an educational leader or planning to take on a leadership role in the K-12 environment. This tool is full of actionable ideas for the mentors, coaches, and administrators dedicated to developing an authentic and dynamic student-centered culture. Mentors who put these strategies in place will make a lasting positive change in the lives of their staff members and their students."

—Joseph Perry,
K-6 STEM Educator
Simmons Elementary School, PA

Student-Centered Mentoring

Student-Centered Mentoring

Keeping Students at the Heart of New Teachers' Learning

Amanda Brueggeman

Foreword by Diane Sweeney

FOR INFORMATION:

Corwin
A SAGE Company
2455 Teller Road
Thousand Oaks, California 91320
(800) 233-9936
www.corwin.com

SAGE Publications Ltd.
1 Oliver's Yard
55 City Road
London EC1Y 1SP
United Kingdom

SAGE Publications India Pvt. Ltd.
B 1/I 1 Mohan Cooperative Industrial Area
Mathura Road, New Delhi 110 044
India

SAGE Publications Asia-Pacific Pte. Ltd.
18 Cross Street #10-10/11/12
China Square Central
Singapore 048423

President: Mike Soules
Vice President and
  Editorial Director: Monica Eckman
Executive Editor: Tori Mello Bachman
Content Development Editor: Sharon Wu
Editorial Assistant: Nancy Chung
Project Editor: Amy Schroller
Copy Editor: Karin Rathert
Typesetter: C&M Digitals (P) Ltd.
Indexer: Integra
Cover Designer: Scott Van Atta
Marketing Manager: Margaret O'Connor

Printed in Canada

Library of Congress Cataloging-in-Publication Data

Names: Brueggeman, Amanda, author.

Title: Student-centered mentoring : keeping students at the heart of new teachers' learning / Amanda Brueggeman.

Description: Thousand Oaks, California : Corwin, 2022. | Series: Corwin teaching essentials; vol. 1 | Includes bibliographical references and index.

Identifiers: LCCN 2021059535 | ISBN 9781071855195 (paperback) | ISBN 9781071876428 (epub) | ISBN 9781071876435 (epub) | ISBN 9781071876442 (pdf)

Subjects: LCSH: Mentoring in education. | Student-centered learning. | Individualized instruction. | First year teachers. | Teacher-student relationships.

Classification: LCC LB1731.4 .B78 2022 | DDC 371.102—dc23/eng/20220110
LC record available at https://lccn.loc.gov/2021059535

This book is printed on acid-free paper.

22 23 24 25 26 10 9 8 7 6 5 4 3 2 1

CONTENTS

For additional resources related to
*Student-Centered Mentoring: Keeping Students
at the Heart of New Teachers' Learning,*
please visit the companion website at
resources.corwin.com/studentcenteredmentoring

FOREWORD

We are at a crossroads. We can either bring talented teachers into the workforce and support them in meaningful ways, or we can continue down the path of looming teacher turnover and shortages. According to a report from the Economic Policy Institute, "A lack of sufficient, qualified teachers threatens students' ability to learn (Darling-Hammond 1999; Ladd and Sorensen 2016). Instability in a school's teacher workforce (i.e., high turnover and/or high attrition) negatively affects student achievement and diminishes teacher effectiveness and quality" (Garcia and Weiss, 2019).

Student-Centered Mentoring by Amanda Brueggeman reimagines how we serve and support teachers entering the profession. While most educators will tell you that early in their career they received some form of induction or mentoring, the focus is often on things like accessing resources, understanding district programs, and following district procedures. Taking this approach places the students in the background rather than the forefront of mentoring conversations. We can do better. What if mentoring also focused on creating classrooms where students learned at the highest levels? This book frames that vision by answering the following questions.

How can we think more broadly about mentee support so that it addresses student learning as well as teachers' emotional needs, communication strategies, physical aspects of the classroom, and instructional practice?

If we think of new teachers as empty vessels to be filled, then we are missing the point. Rather, they are members of our community who need multifaceted systems of support. These layers of support include shared learning, building a collective mindset, opportunities for observational learning, and providing mentees with in-depth support across the year. Throughout the book, these layers are expanded upon in order to provide methods and strategies for this important work.

How do Student-Centered Coaching and Student-Centered Mentoring compare?

In the first chapter of the book, Brueggeman compares Student-Centered Coaching with Student-Centered Mentoring. While they are built on the same philosophical footing, they do serve different purposes, which makes these distinctions important. For example, she suggests that the mentor is the primary support for the mentee throughout the year. They collaborate regularly and may even partner together in a coaching cycle. The coach, on the other hand, is charged with partnering with all teachers in the school, and this may include facilitating coaching cycles, team meetings, informal planning support, and other instructional coaching work.

How do we take care of mentees while at the same time helping them take care of their students?

If we integrate a student-centered philosophy into our thinking about mentoring, then we will be better able to design our work to impact the lives of our students. For example, when working with a mentee, do we keep an eye on how specific teaching behaviors are impacting student learning? Do we use student evidence to confirm our theories about what best practice might look like in any given classroom? Are we able to purposefully connect teaching and learning? These practices will inevitably lead to a more Student-Centered Mentoring program. Even more importantly, they will set up new teachers with the tools they'll need to be sure every decision they make is in the best interest of their students.

What if we applied the practices for Student-Centered Coaching to a mentoring context?

While Student-Centered Coaching is typically implemented broadly across a school, there are ways we can use coaching cycles to support mentees. For example, in Chapter 6, the author recommends partnering mentors and mentees in coaching cycles. This provides the opportunity to collaborate together when establishing a standards-based goal, developing success criteria, and co-planning lessons. The coach then co-teaches in both classrooms, serving as a bridge between the mentor and mentee. This allows the mentor and mentee to build a culture of collective efficacy as they learn from one another while being guided by the coach.

In Closing

It's been ten years since I first met Amanda. At the time, she was a fourth-grade teacher and I was working with her district's team of literacy coaches. We were looking for a classroom where we could practice our coaching moves, and when I asked if there might be a teacher who we could recruit for this purpose, one of the coaches suggested her. We spent the afternoon collecting student evidence and practicing our co-teaching strategies with her students. A few years later, I wasn't surprised when she became a literacy coach herself. Later, as Amanda worked to earn her doctorate, she chose to focus her research on how mentoring could be a more student-centered endeavor, leading to this book. More recently, she has joined our team of coaching consultants.

The progression that Amanda went through as she grappled with how to most effectively mentor new teachers is the same process that I went through decades ago as I struggled to coach in a way that impacted teacher and student learning. She and I share the belief that we must find ways to provide differentiated and needs-based support to teachers at all stages of their careers. *Student-Centered Mentoring* not only provides useful strategies, it is grounded in a set of beliefs that are about meeting new teachers where they are and offering just what they need to brave the inevitable storms of being a new teacher.

—Diane Sweeney

Author of: *The Essential Guide for Student-Centered Coaching* (2020), *Leading Student-Centered Coaching* (2018), *Student-Centered Coaching: The Moves* (2017), and *Student-Centered Coaching from a Distance* (2021)

ACKNOWLEDGMENTS

Mentors are in every aspect of life, both personal and professional. Some of us have a never-ending list, and some only have a few. Either way, a mentor supports, assists, encourages, listens, and does so many other actions that make a difference.

To my many, many mentors—I would not be where I am today without the guidance and support of so many special people in my life. So I am going to try my best to acknowledge as many as I can now.

To my mom and dad—From before I was born, you all have been preparing to raise me in an environment where I can thrive. You both did without, on more than one occasion, to make that happen. Thank you for being my first models of love and care. Thank you for instilling the work ethic and persistence I have depended on time and time again. Mom—I know you are still guiding me as you look down on me from heaven. I continue to hear your voice in the back of my mind day after day. Dad—I still look up to you in how you pour your heart and soul into your farming passion. Just as I admired your will from the time I was little, I will keep watching you be the amazing role model you are!

To my husband—I am so thankful to have you by my side. I appreciate the slack you pick up, without hesitation. Thank you for loving me even in my stressful moments. Thank you for caring for me when I was exhausted from the many hours of writing. And thank you for feeding me even when I thought I was almost done for the day . . . and then an hour later you would still be waiting on me. Thank you for sometimes just bringing me ice cream for dinner!

To my siblings—Matt and Lauren, thank you for letting me spoil your children. I love them as they were my own, and you never say no when I want to visit them. They are my biggest "whys" for wanting to impact so many students in the world. Thank you for the inspiration as I watch you all raise such awesome humans! Lesley—I am so glad to call you a sister. Thank you for the encouragement you give me in following my dreams.

To Kristina—You are my sounding board. Where would I be without our calls? I appreciate the editor you have been for many of my projects and original work years before this book. Thank you for pushing me to keep going, no matter what. Most of all, thank you for our friendship.

To my Valley Park colleagues—You all were my beginning mentors and helped me get my start in teaching. Laura McCoy—I am proud I was able to be your student teacher and then colleague. Thank you for showing me the ropes as I began my teaching career.

To my Wentzville Colleagues—There are so many of you! I am so very lucky to work with such knowledgeable and empowering educators. Margo Mann and my coaching team—you all are why I love literacy! Thank you to each of you and the inspiration you all provide me along my journey as an educator. Dr. Karen Hill—your partnership in trying the mentoring work has been integral in this book and I will be forever grateful. Diane Nanney—you are the epitome of a mentor to me and I am blessed to have been on your team when I first came to the district. Thank you for being my "buddy" early on in my career. Thank you for our continued friendship. Teachers and principals of the many Wentzville Elementaries—I am lucky to work alongside so many hard-working people. Thank you for your passion in teaching our community. And thank you for letting me be a partner with you along the way.

To my consulting teammates—I am extremely lucky to work with you all! Diane Sweeney—you recognized my abilities as a coach, and now I am a part of your team. I would not have written this book if it wasn't for you pushing me outside of my comfort zone! Thank you for telling me I was onto something. And thank you for believing in me! Joy—thank you for partnering with me on several presentations and now being a lifelong friend as well. Rachel—thank you for our brainstorming sessions and letting me "virtually" visit with your kids. Thank you to my other teammates for also supporting this work and lending thoughts along the way!

PUBLISHERS ACKNOWLEDGMENTS

Corwin gratefully acknowledges the contributions of the following reviewers:

Megan Abramczyk, Administrative Intern
Francis Howell School District
St. Charles, MO

Carla Boulton, Education Program Consultant
FBLA-PBL, Inc.
La Center, KY

Andrea Brown-Thirston, CEO & Founder
Optimal Learning Solutions LLC
Homewood, IL

JM Eitner
Commissioner of Education
Laurel, NJ

Sarah Valter, Literacy Coordinator
Lindberg Schools,
St. Louis, MO

Jigisha Vyas, Instructional Coach
Wycoff Public Schools
Fair Lawn, NJ

Crystal Wash, President
Consortium for Educational Research and Advancement
Chicago, IL

ABOUT THE AUTHOR

Amanda Brueggeman, EdD, is a literacy coach and consultant with over 17 years in education. She grew up on a farm in Southeast Missouri and then worked her way to the suburbs of St. Louis, where she taught at Valley Park and Wentzville for ten years prior to being a coach. Amanda holds her doctorate of education in teacher leadership from Maryville University, where she is also currently an adjunct professor for the education department. An area she is passionate about is collective efficacy in relation to working with students, teachers, instructional coaches, and pre-service teachers. In her free time, Amanda enjoys spending time with her husband, Jay, and hanging out with friends, as well as traveling to see family.

INTRODUCTION

BELIEFS ARE AT OUR CORE

The beliefs we hold are the cornerstone of what you say and the actions you take. Our mindset can be heavily guarded because we tend to fall back on our experiences and cultural background from childhood until our most recent life moments. Some of these experiences are effective, and some, well, should probably be forgotten. Either way, as humans we can be very passionate about what our brains and hearts hold on to. Teachers are no different. Although educators are especially heartfelt in our joy of being around students and our passion to build their love for learning, there is no getting around the fact that our beliefs impact our instructional practices.

For over fifteen years, I have worked directly with beginning teachers, teacher mentors, students, and administrators supporting the development of educators as they build and refine their instructional practices and effectiveness in the classroom. My experience has helped me realize that there are four core beliefs that are fundamental to my success:

1. I believe empowering others to grow and make an impact on students is important for our future.

2. I believe learning is a process and so is teaching. You cannot have one without the other.

3. I believe in relying on others, our knowledge, and our experiences to help brave life's storms and see the beauty in those storms, too.

4. I believe in setting goals and being prepared to try again and again and again, both personally and professionally.

What do you believe? Let's begin our work as mentors by taking a journey down memory lane and thinking back to the experiences that have shaped our beliefs. As you read about my four core belief statements, consider the questions I pose to help you form thoughts of your own.

I believe empowering others to grow and make an impact on students is important for our future.

Think about a former student who you've seen years after having them in your class. Maybe they came back to visit you in your classroom, or you passed them at the grocery store or a restaurant. The moment they ask if you remember who they are, you have trouble containing yourself. Of course, you remember! You probably remember their seat in the classroom, how they behaved socially or academically, and maybe even who their best friend was. You may also remember the rituals, songs, books read, or even symbols or visuals that helped that student learn. Despite how old you feel when they say their age, you immediately hope for their continued success.

As I write this, one of my most memorable classes is about to graduate from high school. They were the class I looped with; the class that I formed relationships with like no other because of the extended time we were together. Now, I see them making life decisions and succeeding, in big and small ways. Those fourth- and fifth-grade classrooms may have been years ago, but the memories of them come flooding back whenever I see Facebook posts from those students about their upcoming graduation and college decisions. I remember their group presentations about the weather and the important conversations we had about how to encourage each other to speak in front of the class. I also remember the vulnerable discussions we had about divorce while reading *Hatchet*, where time just seemed to get away from us. Those memories remind me of my commitment—to keep student learning at the forefront of my thinking and actions. No matter how big or small, the symbols or rituals we implore will impact their memory more than we may ever know. Because if remembering those times gives me hope, passion, and purpose, I can only wonder what my past students recall that could be empowering to them.

As you reflect on this core belief, consider these questions:

1. What learning experiences can you recall with your students, as a student, at school, and/or at home?

2. Do you have symbols or rituals that stand out from your childhood and/or years of teaching?

I believe learning is a process and so is teaching. You cannot have one without the other.

If I ever say again to my husband, "I want to go back to get another degree," he would be inclined to say no. I guarantee our bank account would look a lot different without all of my school loans! But despite the fact that I think I am done earning degrees, I have found other learning opportunities and can without a doubt say I still have more to learn in life.

As a literacy coach, one learning area I am still developing is my knowledge of phonics development in the younger grades. My teaching background was mostly upper elementary, so I have had to really push myself to learn how to support teachers and learners in the area of foundational reading skills. It has been a focus of mine for several years, and yet I still learn more with each webinar or book I read.

I have also learned to be okay with vulnerability. Over the years, my willingness to attempt something I know nothing about in front of others has increased both as an educator and in my personal life. For example, I have spent the last three years learning to lift weights properly, and I'll let you in on a little secret, I actually kind of enjoy it now! But when I first started, I was a nervous wreck when someone other than my husband would watch me lift because my form was far from perfect. However, coming to grips with vulnerability has helped me become the teacher I am today. I have learned that perfection does not occur every time, and I must work to model quality practices and performance both professionally and personally, which includes vulnerability.

As you reflect on this core belief, consider these questions:

1. What skills and attributes do you believe are needed to teach all learners?

2. How do you view learning for yourself and all students?

I believe in relying on others, our knowledge, and our experiences to help brave life's storms and see the beauty in those storms, too.

From an early age, my parents taught me to leave a legacy of collectiveness. When I was in my twenties, my mom passed away. However, her impact on my growth as a person still continues. She was known for being so helpful, giving great advice, and pushing others to work for a cause. In the end, she shaped the lives of countless individuals. I want to be remembered like that. I want to find the good in a situation or a solution to a problem. Rather than choosing to let something get me down, I want to grow. But I know I cannot do that alone.

That is why I am committed to promoting a positive and collaborative school culture. Currently, our world is balancing positive versus negative as we work to recover from the effects of COVID-19. I have witnessed colleagues work together and many find the best opportunities in the virtual experiences. I have found myself spending more time learning through webinars and reading more, but I also have found a new love for Twitter and online meetings. Technology has allowed me to form and maintain connections to other educators across the country, like my Diane Sweeney Consulting Group and Teachers College Staff Developers. I will be able to depend on these relationships for many years to come. If living through a pandemic can teach our world anything, it is that working together to achieve a better world is the puzzle piece that could make the biggest difference in bringing people together. And it is this same mindset that is key for Student-Centered Mentoring—we have to work together as a team and be supportive to grow our impact.

As you reflect on this core belief, consider these questions:

1. Who has influenced your life and in what ways?

2. What peer interactions can you remember that resulted in important learning experiences?

I believe in setting goals and being prepared to try again and again and again, both personally and professionally.

I am sometimes afraid of a challenge and what change can bring, like being afraid of a storm and its aftermath. Those last moments I sat by my mom's hospital bed were consumed with thoughts of how unsure I was about life without her. As time has passed, I remember moments with her—like when she helped me organize my classroom library on several occasions. That classroom library was always a daunting task to me, and I never felt I got it perfect, but I kept trying. I even remember being encouraged to apply for a literacy coach position and thinking, "If I struggle with arranging a classroom library, how can I even be remotely qualified to be a literacy coach!" But instead of consuming my thoughts with "I can't," I chose to set a goal to learn more and capitalize on my strengths that could instead help teachers and students. I leaned on the guidance of many to assist in that work, as well as many other learning moments.

After a year as literacy coach, I decided to get my doctorate. It was a high achieving goal and one in which I depended on the advice of my husband, family, and colleagues in order to fully invest in attempting. There were times that I had to redo a project or get feedback to make something better, but in the end, that time and energy helped me grow in my coaching position. Revising my goals after receiving constructive feedback and advice has also been important in my personal growth—which are characteristics I learned from my mom and others who have supported me along the way. All of this learning has opened doors to other opportunities, like consulting, that makes me proud to spread the knowledge of Student-Centered Coaching and Student-Centered Mentoring to others around the country in order to impact even more students' learning. This is why I am committed to accepting challenges and working collaboratively toward making an impact. I know my mom would want me to continue to follow my passion to teach and collectively do what is right for students—never giving up, even when it might become tough.

As you reflect on this core belief, consider these questions:

1. What is your learning identity that helps you to achieve your goals—preferred style, methods, and passions?

2. What are the qualities of your most notable mentors?

UNCOVER YOUR EDUCATIONAL BELIEFS

The four beliefs I shared have come to fruition over my lifetime of experiences and are the core values of *Student-Centered Mentoring*. Ultimately, an underlying purpose of choosing to serve rather than looking for appreciation was the reason I developed this approach. It is my hope that *Student-Centered Mentoring* will guide your journey to a similar purpose and make your role of mentoring a little easier. In addition, think about how you can challenge others to consider their beliefs as they learn about Student-Centered Mentoring and even adjust their values to develop their mindset. To help you with that work, here (Figure 1.1) is a summary of the questions connected to each of my beliefs.

Figure 1.1 Summary of Belief Questions

What Are Your Educational Beliefs?
1. What learning experiences can you recall with your students, as a student, at school, and/or at home?
2. Do you have symbols or rituals that stand out from your childhood and/or years of teaching?
3. What skills and attributes do you believe are needed for teaching all learners?
4. How do you view learning for yourself and all students?
5. Who has influenced your life and in what ways?
6. What peer interactions can you remember that resulted in important learning experiences?
7. What is your learning identity that helps you to achieve your goals—preferred style, methods, passions?
8. What are the qualities of your most notable mentors?

MENTOR TIP

Using your responses to the belief questions, develop a list of your core belief statements around educational practices.

WHAT IS STUDENT-CENTERED MENTORING?

Student-Centered Mentoring is a collaborative approach for mentors and mentees that focuses heavily on the impact of students' learning using the layers of support in progression from foundational to in-the-moment learning (Figure 1.2). Traditional mentoring differs in that it concentrates the support and professional learning solely on teachers growing expertise in their content area. It can often be viewed as more evaluative and focused on teacher actions rather than student outcomes.

Student-Centered Mentoring

- Collaboration around the impact of instruction on students' learning

Traditional Mentoring

- Teacher-centered focus on mentee's actions and content area

Figure 1.2 Layers of Student-Centered Mentoring

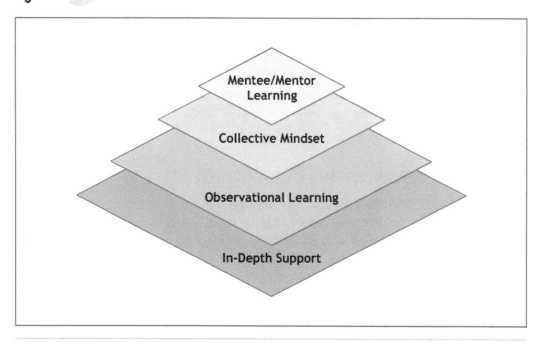

MENTEE/MENTOR LEARNING

The first layer encompasses the start of many beginning teacher programs using a student-centered approach. Most new teacher programs primarily showcase teacher-centered methods, so it is a shift in information and processes to be inclusive of a student-centered lens. This layer focuses on the time spent with mentees before walking into their first day of school but is also incorporated into the continuous work you engage in with your mentee throughout the year. Mentor learning is also integral because it has been shown that teacher retention increases when mentors receive support as well.

COLLECTIVE MINDSET

Student-Centered Mentoring is more than just a structure to support new teachers and mentors; it is also a shift in our educational mindset. This next layer uses the research behind brain-based learning to promote the mindset and viewpoints that can be most supportive in shifting to a student-centered approach with new teacher programs. Believing in our potential coupled with the fact that our profession is increasing in demand of time and energy brings about the importance of working collectively to make an impact on students. Additionally, providing a format for collaborative reflection and goal-setting conversations is pertinent for building an effective mentee/mentor partnership. This will then help increase collective efficacy with the mentee/mentor as well as with the instructional coach, administrators, and other staff.

OBSERVATIONAL LEARNING

All educators find value in watching others learn. So why not have mentors and new teachers learn together as well as from each other. The third layer of support makes student learning visible to new teachers and mentors in a joint setting. Multiple observation options can be used where individuals as well as other colleagues and administrators can have a visual understanding of teaching practices. Whether the new teacher observes their mentor or the two of them visit another host classroom the learning is extended to more than just the beginning teacher. The mentor and new teacher duo provides empowerment and accountability in the partnership.

IN-DEPTH SUPPORT

The last layer of support incorporates Student-Centered Coaching into the new teacher and mentor partnership. Mentor Coaching Cycles are instructional coaching cycles that include both the mentee and mentor and focus on the students from both classrooms. Coaching, in general, provides teachers with in-the-moment learning centered on increasing the effect of their instructional practices. Mentor Coaching Cycles creates a triad collaboration team that encourages not only new teachers but also mentors in going from surface to deep learning.

WHY STUDENT-CENTERED MENTORING?

There are four key characteristics for providing a tiered system of learning through the lens of students: support, impact, mind frame, and growth.

SUPPORT

Teaching is hard. The support of colleagues is what makes teaching a little bit easier. At the end of a hard day, many teachers rely on conversations with colleagues and encouragement to keep going. Relating back to my beliefs, I am reminded of the many mentors in my life who have given me guidance as an educator and who took time out of their days to help me.

The collective mindset approach is what provides a supportive atmosphere for beginning teachers and their students to grow and learn. It is often that support comes in the form of encouragement when you're having a challenging day. Through the support of mentors, we can realize that trying a new lesson or strategy or reading the way students respond in their learning is far more important than having perfect execution. Having the support of colleagues and mentors can help us take instructional risks and be far more affective when we take care of ourselves as well.

IMPACT

My hope for Student-Centered Mentoring is to have a broader impact on *all* students. It is evident that educators want to see students grow and succeed, but that takes time. In the same token, teachers' growth takes time. Some instructional practices are also more effective to use than others. This is where it is important to understand how students learn and how to develop students' independence as drivers of their own learning. Rather than asking, "What content should I teach?" we should be asking, "How can I prepare students to problem-solve when learning gets hard?" If we take this approach with beginning teachers, then maybe we can empower more educators and students to impact our world for the better.

MIND FRAME

In order to support mentees and mentors, we have to believe in the mentoring partnerships' abilities to make substantial impact on students' learning. "How we think about the impact of what we do is more important than what we do" (Hattie, 2018, ix). If we think we can help students learn, then we have the mindset that will make that possible. Rather, if we think a student is incapable, then it is likely that the student will not grow or learn like other students. Anyone who has worked with students and teachers knows that there are people in both groups who can seem closed off to learning new things. Whether uncertain or just reluctant, the common chord is often a discomfort with vulnerability and stepping outside of their comfort zone. Although it's not easy to change, we must work with students and teachers to make progressive mindset shifts.

GROWTH

It takes time to grow in our practice. It takes time to see the growth in students and their learning. Are there always going to be challenges to face? Yes, of course. Some will be big, and some will be small. Some will be simple, and some will be complex. Some will need anyone to help, and some will be about finding the *right* people to help. In the end, growth is possible. We have to learn to overcome challenges by accepting the changes, learning from them, and continuing to work toward impacting students. If we attempt to be innovators, we truly embody the vulnerability it takes to grow. "To develop students as 'innovators' in their pursuits, we must embody this as educators," (Couros, 2014). Therefore, it is important to model for our students what it takes to learn new things. This is one of the primary purposes of *Student-Centered Mentoring*, to ultimately help new teachers and mentors and ultimately students to all become innovators.

HOW TO APPROACH *STUDENT-CENTERED MENTORING*

The chapters in this book are organized by the layers of Student-Centered Mentoring (See Figure I.3). Each chapter provides strategies mentors can use to support their work with mentees and includes tips and action steps to assist in implementation. The "In The Classroom" strategies throughout the book can be used with mentors and mentees as well as with students. The power behind this useful tool adds another avenue to being student-centered! You can choose which chapter to read based on the layer or the specific strategies you may want to focus on. If you are new to the concept of Student-Centered Mentoring, I recommend starting with the first and second layer.

Figure 1.3 Organization of This Book

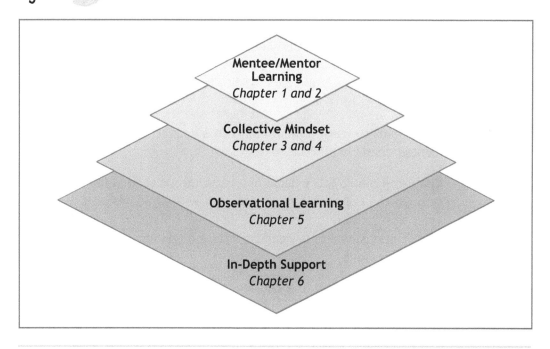

FOCUS ON MENTEE/MENTOR LEARNING

Chapter 1 uncovers the meaning of Student-Centered Mentoring and compares it to a traditional teacher-centered approach. This chapter not only guides mentors in how to incorporate Student-Centered Mentoring with their mentees but also leads an exploration of a student-centered environment in their own classrooms.

If you want to learn more about taking a student-centered approach with beginning teachers, read Chapter 1.

Chapter 2 provides a foundation for professional learning, both for the new teacher and the mentor in beginning their partnership. A positive relationship is key to the Student-Centered Mentoring approach. Some of the knowledge consists of listening to the needs of new teachers and guiding mentees to listen to their students. Forming appropriate feedback is included here, as it is a large part of a mentor's role in an effective partnership.

If you want to boost your learning as a mentor and learn how to begin a successful mentor/mentee partnership, read Chapter 2.

FOCUS ON COLLECTIVE MINDSET

Chapter 3 goes into the efficacy shaping of both new teachers and their mentors, allowing for exploration of innovative learning mindsets in conjunction with brain-based learning. This chapter also takes a deep look at mind frames, as they are essential to a teacher's continual development and their ability to make an impact on students from the start of their career.

If you want to learn how to embrace a collective mindset with your mentee, read Chapter 3.

Chapter 4 employs the heart of what it means to be a teacher today, through the collaborative partnership with colleagues. It also provides a structured format for collaborative reflection and goal-setting conversations, which is significant for a beginning teacher and mentor's relationship.

If you want to promote a continued partnership with new teachers, read Chapter 4.

FOCUS ON OBSERVATIONAL LEARNING

Chapter 5 builds the repertoire of experiences for both the beginning teacher and the mentor by providing clarity of instructional practices with ideas for observation. This chapter explains how the mentor and teacher duo promotes empowerment and provides accountability within observational learning.

If you want ideas for on-the-spot experiences to support instructional practices and observations, read Chapter 5.

FOCUS ON IN-DEPTH SUPPORT

Chapter 6 focuses on how to structure Mentor Coaching Cycles using the Student-Centered Coaching model. This chapter discusses the powerful benefits of developing a mentor and mentee's collective efficacy through a joint coaching cycle and practicing on-the-spot learning with a focus on students.

If you want information about coaching support for your mentee/ mentor partnership, read Chapter 6.

CONCLUSION

It is now time for your Student-Centered Mentoring journey to begin. As you continue reading, keep your beliefs at the forefront. Just remember, it is also a part of the journey for your beliefs to grow. It is more than acceptable to adjust those beliefs as you gain further experience and knowledge through your time as a mentor and even more so as an educator.

SHIFTING TOWARD A STUDENT-CENTERED APPROACH

Imagine it's the first day of school. If what you're picturing is anything like the photos I often see floating around social media, you are perfectly dressed, your hair is well styled, and your classroom is neat and organized as students begin swarming into the school. The end of the day, however, looks drastically different. Your hair is a mess and you are slumped over a chair unable to move from sheer exhaustion. The adrenaline from the day has definitely worn off!

How many of you can relate? Each year, I would spend the days and weeks leading up to the first day of school getting ready. I always thought I was prepared. But inevitably I felt like I had been through the ringer on day one, especially my first few years. No matter how prepared I felt, the first day was just exhausting, and my survival instincts would quickly take over. I even remember asking myself, "Can I make a difference with students if every day is like this?"

Now, let's consider the first full year of teaching as a whole. I have met many new teachers where the majority of days for the entire year were like the first day just described. Unfortunately, many educators choose to leave the profession because of too many of these overly demanding days. As a result, I find myself asking questions such as, is it possible to create experiences for new teachers that are more supportive of the increasing demands of a teacher in today's classroom? Are we helping to build teachers' skillsets so that they can confidently send their students to the next grade level knowing students have learned and made appropriate growth? And more importantly, if we shifted our approach to new-teacher induction and mentoring to be more focused on student learning would that build teacher capacity and keep teachers in the profession longer?

WHAT IS THIS CHAPTER ABOUT?

In this chapter, you will learn strategies to

➤ Inquire about the availability of resources for you and your mentee

➤ Integrate a student-centered philosophy into your thinking

➤ Utilize a student-centered method in your mentoring approach

I will review the current status of most teacher induction and mentor programs and will seek to explain why teachers leave the education profession early on in their careers. I will also share definitions for a "new teacher" and the characteristics for being an effective "mentor." Additionally, we will explore teacher-centered and student-centered approaches to mentoring in the areas of instruction, coaching, and induction and learn strategies to help promote teacher retention.

MENTOR INQUIRY PRE-REFLECTION

Use these guiding questions as you explore the ideas in this chapter.

1. What is the current state of new teacher induction in your school or district?

2. How would you define Student-Centered Mentoring?

3. In what areas can you shift your mentoring moves to embrace a more student-centered approach?

WHO IS A NEW TEACHER?

It is natural to think of a new teacher as someone in their first year of teaching. Realistically though, a teacher can be "new" for more than just a year, as it is often situational. For the purposes of this work, let's define a new teacher or a mentee as someone who could fall into any of the following areas:

➤ A beginning teacher in their first year

➤ A second- or even third-year teacher

➤ A teacher new to a district

➤ A reentry teacher

The first two categories above are fairly straightforward. So, let's address the other two categories to see more clearly why those two groups of teachers who might appear to be more experienced can still benefit from a mentor experience.

I can recall when I moved to my current district. I was about to begin my fourth year of teaching but felt as though I was starting all over again. I was concerned about how to do my job in a new place. After a few days of professional learning focused on grade-level content and the physical details of the school district, my brain felt like mush. It was so much new information. I hardly remember anything from the four professional training days that followed. I sat through all the sessions and walked away with ideas, but I was incapable of remembering all of the information being thrown at me. It was just assumed that with my years of experience, I should transition easily. In hindsight, I realized two things: (1) I actually fit into one of the new teacher categories and should have given myself a bit more grace with my learning experience, and (2) the structure of the professional learning was teacher centered. This raises the question—would I have felt more prepared with a student-centered approach to the learning experience?

Each year, there are teachers who reenter the profession after spending time away. Two common scenarios for this are a teacher who returns after raising their family or after caring for a sick or elderly family member. Depending on the circumstances, these teachers could have been absent from the profession for a couple years or maybe even over a decade. The assumption is often that because these teachers have taught before, they have the knowledge and capability to get back into the classroom easily. While that may be true for some, the way education evolves in relation to our ever-changing world can make an impact on a teacher reentering the classroom, even after only a year of leave. Whether it is new instructional standards or assessments, advances in technology, a focus on cultural and emotional learning, or any other new district/school initiatives, reentry teachers need just as much, if not more, support as a new teacher who just finished their undergraduate education.

MENTOR TIP

As you learn more about Student-Centered Mentoring, keep in mind the type of new teacher your mentee may be in order to support their needs effectively.

WHY TEACHERS LEAVE THE PROFESSION

"Why did most of the students not understand my lesson?" "If I could just get the students to listen . . . " "How do I help all of my students?" I can recall my first years of teaching, having that overloaded feeling. From the start of setting up my classroom, I was wishing for the right answers to miraculously help me make a difference with my students. To add to the struggles, I knew that I needed to focus on developing strong instructional practices as well as classroom management skills. And like many new teachers, my students' achievement was lower despite my best efforts.

Approximately half of new teachers in the United States leave the profession within the first five to seven years (Boogren, 2015). These teachers report frustration that the school leadership under supported or undervalued them; stress related to workload, expectations, or number of responsibilities; and anxiety regarding lack of expertise among the reasons why they choose to change professions (Boogren, 2015, p. 11). Many beginning teachers are just taking one day at a time trying to teach their students. How many of you can relate?

In her book, *Supporting Beginning Teachers,* Boogren (2015) details six phases a new teacher goes through. They are (1) anticipation, (2) survival, (3) disillusionment, (4) rejuvenation, (5) reflection, and (6) second anticipation. These phases are essentially like a roller coaster ride. Every teacher starts off the year in anticipation and excitement, but new teachers are more likely to move into the phase of survival or disillusionment pretty quickly. Teachers new to a district, especially first-year teachers, are on information overload from the start and often struggle with low efficacy as they are bombarded with learning how the district works, how their particular building operates, their grade-level curriculum, and running their own classroom. Most schools provide some new teacher training. It could be from professional development chairs, instructional coaches, or administrators prior to school starting. Some teachers get something from all of those individuals. It is also possible that new teacher sessions are spaced throughout the school year, with many being held monthly after school. These sessions traditionally incorporate information required by state guidelines. Any or all of that is necessary, but it is a lot for a first-year teacher.

MENTOR TIP

Watch for signs of struggles with your mentee as well as other peer teachers that could initiate their departure from teaching.

If you see a new teacher begin to struggle, consider the following questions:

▶ Are their beliefs affecting their practices in such a way that lowers their self-confidence?

▶ Are they missing the passion of serving others?

> Are the professional development sessions full of teacher-centered practices rather than a balance that includes more of a focus on student learning?

> Is there a low level of collective efficacy or lack of collaborative culture within the school?

STRATEGIES TO BEGIN USING A STUDENT-CENTERED APPROACH

As mentors, you have the potential to provide the most support for beginning teachers by using a student-centered approach. Taking on a student-centered perspective requires some forethought.

> Raising children who are hopeful and who have the courage to be vulnerable means stepping back and letting them experience disappointment, deal with conflict, learn how to assert themselves, and have the opportunity to fail. If we're always following our children into the arena, hushing the critics, and assuring their victory, they'll never learn that they have the ability to dare greatly on their own.
>
> —Brown (2012) in *Daring Greatly*

You are a key player in helping new teachers to be successful in teaching their students to be independent. These strategies will uncover how you can support them. Strategies one, three, and four include action steps that you can take as you shift into using a student-centered approach.

STRATEGY #1: ESTABLISH THE CURRENT STATUS OF LEARNING SUPPORT

In order to begin our work as mentors, we need to understand the support options for both our mentee and ourselves. What is the current state of the induction programs for mentees specifically? What learning is available by your own school system for you as a mentor? Are the opportunities for learning separate, joint, or a blended model?

ACTION STEP #1: RESEARCH THE CURRENT STATE OF YOUR BEGINNING TEACHER PROGRAM

What is the current approach in your school or district when it comes to the beginning teacher induction? First, you need to be aware of all the people involved in directing mentee work and those who are expected to support your mentee. Often, each group is thought about in silos. New teachers are in one silo. If mentors are present, like you may be, you are a separate silo. The trend continues with other groups, administrators, and so forth, who interact within the system of professional development support of beginning teachers. Why do I compare the groups to silos? When I first began as a teacher, everyone leading my new teacher sessions was compartmentalized. It was the same when I began working with new teachers. Mentors had a half-day session to review the mentoring structure and requirements for their mentee to complete.

Another example of a silo approach is that mentees and mentors often have separate learning sessions in many districts. For example, many schools will hold beginning teacher meetings only for mentees to attend. Many of those sessions also only take place at the start of the year with just beginning teachers. Another possibility is that in larger school systems, administrators may have a slot where they meet their new teachers before school resumes. The same holds true for mentors, where you meet separately with your mentee outside of their induction sessions.

Another possible structure is that mentees and mentors have partnership sessions together. Mentees and mentors may partner in sessions to get to know each other, explore school/district components, learn about their content area, or develop their understanding of instructional practices. This structure that includes mentors may also be partially used in addition to mentees attending learning sessions on their own.

💡 MENTOR TIP

As you consider the nature of your current induction program, take some time to look into the professional learning topics provided to your mentee. It will help you to align support with the information your mentee learns in their beginning teacher sessions.

Once you understand how your district/system is organized, you can look at the actual information that your mentee is learning during their professional development sessions. This will provide windows of opportunity to match up your mentoring support with what your mentee is learning. Keep in mind that the tendency of induction programs is usually teacher centered in nature, where the focus is on understanding the content, district expectations, resources, instruction and curriculum guidelines, and so forth. It may also be that incoming teachers need to attend professional learning through an outside organization. Usually, this is a state certification requirement, and you can help your mentee look into the options in your area. As you read further, you can brainstorm ideas about how to expand your mentee's learning in more of a student-centered approach.

ACTION STEP #2: EXPLORE YOUR MENTOR-LEARNING OPTIONS

It is unrealistic to think that a new teacher could be prepared for the classroom just by reading a manual. The same is true for you as a mentor. The process of training beginning teachers requires collaborative support systems where mentors and mentees can work together to support and learn from each other. As a mentor, you are provided as a counterpart to new teachers and the person who can truly guide them through the hard job of teaching. It is appropriate to ask for guidance in your learning and seek ways to be an effective mentor, especially if that is a new role for you. Seek out your administrators, other mentors, and instructional coaches. Simply ask what resources are available to you as a mentor in your school or district. The next suggestion is to ask about the collaboration or plan time options. Then, take the time to do some research through books, webinars, or professional development, as well as meet with your mentee. The high impact professional learning that is most beneficial to mentors has included ways to establish a supportive network, active and supportive listening, celebrating success, and giving feedback. These strategies have consistently been the top-rated strategies in the mentor rankings of professional learning. The domino effect of support starts with ideas we can use as mentors, to then use with beginning teachers and then possibly with students. This simple step will not only help you to feel more prepared to guide your mentee but can also be a timesaver. Then, be prepared to layer in time for problem-solving conversations focused on students, as well as to observe and learn more as a mentor partnership. Another aspect of time is taking time to grow your relationship. Look ahead to Chapter 2 for ways to do that.

KEEPING IT STUDENT CENTERED

Keep in mind the strategies from this resource that can also be used with students. This means that we approach professional learning with strategies that can be used between a mentor and new teacher, teacher to student, and possibly student to student.

Another key aspect for you to learn is how to promote a student-centered mindset with your mentee. They should be asking themselves questions such as, "What is the best strategy to use for each student?" or "What kind of feedback will be most helpful to students?" Foundational strategies are important to know and understand for any teacher. It is difficult to know where to begin with new teachers in order to not overwhelm them. Looking into how you can provide your mentee with the assistance in their formative years will prove to be a valuable use of your time. You will be empowered to uncover ideas for your mentee and then will want to use these new ideas in your own classroom!

MENTOR TIP

Not sure where to start your own professional learning journey? Find ways to use the professional learning opportunities that are available from this book and anything connected to Visible Learning. Also, look into other possibilities related to the topic of mentoring or supporting beginning teachers. ASCD and Learning Forward are national organizations I have found that offer mentor resources. There are also workshops or print resources by Tina Boogren.

STRATEGY #2: CLARIFY YOUR ROLE AS A MENTOR

Whether you are an aspiring mentor or already in the midst of the job, it is important to understand the details and expectations of the role. If an administrator assigned you, you may have already been told some details of your role. If you are considering a role as a mentor or not yet matched up within a mentoring system, ask how you can partner with a new teacher. Some details to also ask about as a mentor include the following: whether stipends are available to you in this role (depending on funds of course), is there an option to have extra planning periods, or can you alter other job responsibilities due to time constraints. If selected as a mentor, just remember why you have been chosen, which is most likely because you are a teacher leader in the building. Use the bulleted list that follows for a full list of clarifying questions to ask administrators or directors in charge of mentoring:

➤ Is there a mentor and/or mentee handbook?

➤ Are stipends available?

➤ Are extra planning periods possible?

➤ Is substitute teacher coverage available for meetings/observations?

➤ Do other job responsibilities need to be adjusted?

➤ How do you choose mentors?

KEEPING IT STUDENT CENTERED

Providing resources to your mentee is part of the mentoring role but can be more teacher centered. Also, consider these student-centered attributes as you learn more about mentoring beginning teachers using a student-centered approach:

- Teacher leader
- Asked to be a mentor
- Growth and innovative mindset
- Gives strengths-based feedback
- Culturally responsive
- Active listener

If you are aspiring to be a mentor, consider the make-up of your school to understand your possibilities. Who you mentor may depend on the pool of options and school parameters set by administrators. It is natural to pair up with a new colleague in the same content or grade level, but school size may inhibit that. I am a perfect example of that. My mentor was a teacher leader in our building who had just transferred to a technology-coach position. A plus to that pairing was that she saw my strengths in using technology in the classroom and encouraged me to obtain my masters in educational technology. Whether you are a classroom teacher or in another role like my mentor, be sure to communicate the desire to your administrator. Also, be prepared with options for supporting your role, along with questions similar to the topics mentioned throughout the book.

A common question is how the roles of a mentor and an instructional coach are different. Remember from the beginning of the chapter that as the mentor, you are the primary point person for your mentee. Even if there are multiple teammates or colleagues around, a beginning teacher naturally reaches out to their mentor first when they have a question or need advice. An instructional coach would be a secondary person of support. As the mentor, you are the full-time support in collaboration and ongoing work with your mentee. Your classroom is most likely in close proximity, which helps beginning teachers to have better access when needed. The most successful mentorships I have witnessed have times built into their schedules to meet regularly. An instructional coach is spread throughout a building as a form of support for all teachers. The chart in Figure 1.1 compares the typical responsibilities of a mentor and an instructional coach. You can share this with your administrator and instructional coach to guide conversations about the two roles if further clarification is needed.

Figure 1.1 Mentor and Coach Role Comparison

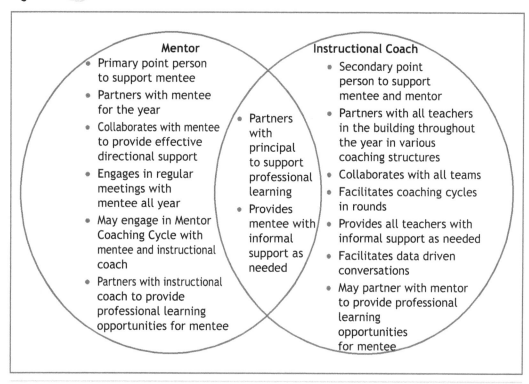

Depending on the needs of your building, you could be an instructional coach asked to take on the role of mentor. If that is the case, it will be important to consider how to balance coaching for all teachers in the building as well as supporting your mentee. If possible, discuss the option to use a different support person to mentor the new teacher(s). Additional rationale for this will be provided later in the chapter when we discuss collective teacher efficacy, but the big idea is that new teachers should have a teaching partner as their mentor, along with others in the building, such as an instructional coach or school counselor, who provide assistance in varying ways.

MENTOR TIP

Don't be afraid to clarify the details and expectations of your mentoring role, especially if there is any confusion or if multiple people work with the new teachers in your building.

STRATEGY #3: INTEGRATE A STUDENT-CENTERED PHILOSOPHY INTO YOUR THINKING

It is time for you to build your background of the student-centered philosophy. I find it most helpful to explore the Student-Centered Coaching model designed by Diane Sweeney to analyze teacher-centered and student-centered approaches. We cannot forget the most important part of thinking student centered, the classroom itself. What student-centered instructional practices can you add to your toolbox?

ACTION STEP #1: EXPLORE TEACHER-CENTERED AND STUDENT-CENTERED COACHING

Sweeney and Harris (2020) define Student-Centered Coaching as an evidence-based instructional coaching model that shifts the focus from "fixing" teachers to collaborating with them to design instruction that targets student outcomes. While your role as a mentor is not exclusive to instructional coaching support, looking through the lens of a Student-Centered Coaching approach will help you better understand the philosophy of Student-Centered Mentoring. This will help you to better support your mentee in their development as a teacher.

KEEPING IT STUDENT CENTERED

I have learned more about mentoring with a student-centered focus through the use of the Student-Centered Coaching model. As you read, note something you have learned about the Student-Centered Coaching structure that will help you grow your view of being student-centered in your mentoring practices.

A teacher-centered coach takes on the role of moving a teacher through a program or set of instructional practices, solely focused on actions of the teacher. The primary role of a student-centered coach is being a partner with the teacher and co-teaching based on a student goal for learning. When I was a classroom teacher, I will never forget my desire to help my fifth-grade students become better writers. I signed up for a coaching cycle and through our work together around a student goal focused on opinion writing, my coach, Amanda Gift, and I saw tremendous growth in my students' learning. I used to think I could never be considered a "writer," and I now believe I became a lover of writing due to our partnership.

Data is also used differently. In a teacher-centered coaching cycle, the coach evaluates the teacher based on student data. A Student-Centered Coaching approach analyzes student evidence to guide next steps and measures the impact on student learning proficiency from the beginning to the end of a cycle. According to a KickUp Study (n.d.) of teachers who participated in Student-Centered Coaching cycles, students' average proficiency levels went from 5% in the pre-assessment to 73% in the post-assessment.

The structures for using instructional tools are also unique. Materials, such as a particular program, are the primary driver for the coach and teacher in a teacher-centered approach, while a student-centered approach focuses more on the learning outcomes desired for the students using the program or other resources as an option for support.

The perception of the coach is also strikingly opposite with these approaches. A teacher-centered coach takes the lead on the work with a teacher and is viewed as the expert. In student-centered coaching, joint collaboration between the coach and the teacher is the key to helping students grow. Taking the stance of learning together is a huge component of the practice of a student-centered approach. It is about working together so that our craft can grow and we can share ideas from teacher to teacher. Figure 1.2 compares the two coaching models.

Figure 1.2 Comparison of Teacher-Centered Versus Student-Centered Coaching

	Teacher-Centered Coaching	Student-Centered Coaching
Role	The coach moves teachers toward implementing a program or set of instructional practices.	The coach partners with teachers to design learning that is based on a specific objective for student learning.
Focus	The focus is on what the teacher is, or is not, doing and addressing it through coaching.	The focus is on using data and student work to analyze progress and collaborate to make informed decisions about instruction that is differentiated and needs-based.
Use of Data	Summative assessment data is used to hold teachers accountable, rather than as a tool for instructional decision making.	Formative assessment data and student work is used to determine how to design the instruction. Summative assessment data is used to assess progress toward standards mastery.
Use of Materials	The use of textbooks, technology, and curricular programs is the primary objective of the coaching.	Textbooks, technology, and curricular programs are viewed as tools for moving student learning to the next level.
Perception of the Coach	The coach is viewed as a person who is there to hold teachers accountable for a certain set of instructional practices.	The coach is viewed as a partner who is there to support teachers to move students toward mastery of the standards.

Printed with permission from Sweeney and Harris (2017)

ACTION STEP #2: BRAINSTORM STUDENT-CENTERED IDEAS TO ADD TO YOUR INSTRUCTIONAL PRACTICES

Education traditionally started as the perfect example of the teacher-centered approach. Teachers were almost always in front of the students sitting in rows. Unfortunately, even hundreds of years later, many classrooms haven't changed from that configuration. Whether the teacher's desk is in the front of the room with rows of student desks or in an arrangement of pods or tables, if students always have the teacher teaching in the front of the room, it is still teacher-centered instruction. In a student-centered classroom, there is a shared focus between both students and teachers. One example of this is in workshop-style classrooms, where the teacher confers with a student or meets with a group of students while the remaining students work around the room. The key idea of any student-centered classroom is that it isn't always obvious where the teacher is and students could be scattered around the room.

IN THE CLASSROOM

Arrange your classroom desks in groups to promote a collaborative environment. If you already arrange your room in pods or tables, consider how you can bring students in on room arrangement. One option could be to incorporate a routine where students are able to pick their seats and partners.

Classroom dialogue is another area where student-centered practices can be incorporated. If the teacher is always the one talking, then it is a monologue or lecture. More than likely, this is also where students are trying to get notes down as fast as possible. The opposite occurs in a student-centered classroom, where the discussion between students and teachers during learning is more about dialogue. Here, student conversations are happening the majority of the time and are highly influential in affecting student achievement. Dialogue is important to be mindful of because it doubles the speed of learning. As with the Visible Learning research, classroom discussion has an effect size of 0.82, which shows that acceleration of student learning through conversation (Visible Learning MetaX, n.d.a). This is based on a 0.4 effect size being equal to a year's worth of growth.

In addition to classroom dialogue, the use of instructional strategies is varied in a student-centered classroom. Strategies that support cooperative learning and collaborative group work are used to guide learning rather than direct instruction and independent work. However, a student-centered environment does not always mean that students work together. It can include students working independently, at times, with the intent of working with other students at some point but not always from the direction of the teacher. This connects back to the use of frequent dialogue, where students and teachers have conversations around learning. An example could be in a writing class where students are working on informational research papers and continuously check in with partners to get feedback throughout the writing process. Figure 1.3 outlines key ideas of using teacher-centered compared to student-centered instruction.

KEEPING IT STUDENT CENTERED

Think about the student-centered instructional techniques you already use in the classroom and brainstorm additional ideas to add to your instructional toolbox.

Figure 1.3 Comparison of Teacher-Centered and Student-Centered Instruction

	Teacher-Centered	Student-Centered
Focus	The focus of attention is on the teacher.	The focus is shared between the students and teachers.
Dialogue	Monologue is used the majority of the time by the teacher.	Students and teachers have conversations around the learning.
Use of Strategies	Teacher primarily uses direct instruction.	Strategies consist of a combination of cooperative learning and collaboration.
Activities	Students work independently with direction from the teacher.	Teachers and students interact equally in pairs or groups.

STRATEGY #4: UTILIZE A STUDENT-CENTERED METHOD FOR MENTORING

When mentoring beginning teachers, it is important to consider the following components:

- Focus of training

- Methods of instruction and assessment

- Follow-up

- Goal setting

- Process

- Depth

As you read further, you will connect the Student-Centered Mentoring philosophy to each of these components. You can use the aspects to promote effective professional learning of all mentees.

ACTION STEP #1: COMPARE TEACHER-CENTERED AND STUDENT-CENTERED INDUCTION APPROACHES

A teacher-centered learning session focuses solely on the teacher and the curriculum content, whereas a student-centered program focuses on student learning and the instructional strategies that should be used. This approach also promotes growth and innovative mindsets, which enables collective efficacy. With an effect size of 1.39, collective efficacy has a powerful influence on students' learning (Visible Learning MetaX, n.d.b).

Goals are another important aspect of professional learning for beginning teachers and can be made with assistance from administrators or mentors in either approach. Teacher-centered methods and content-related information are typically the focus of goal setting in a teacher-centered approach. Conversely, goals around student learning and the use of high expectations are an integral part of a student-centered approach.

Student-centered mentoring includes collaborative meetings and follow-up to any trainings or other potential work centered on the mentee's goals. Conversely, mentors are evaluators of their mentees' delivery of content in a teacher-centered approach. In a student-centered approach, mentors partner with new teachers to analyze their impact on student learning together. The pair collaborates regularly and observes students during learning activities to assist in setting next steps based on the mentee's goals. More so than almost anything, teachers are working toward being change agents for their students and their learning.

In order to go in-depth with any professional learning experience, it is important for teachers to actually be in the classroom and have on-the-spot experiences. In a teacher-centered approach, new teachers may observe other teachers, primarily you as the mentor as well as at random in the building, district, or other locations. They also may or may not have a focus within those observations around the teacher-centered goals. This differs from a student-centered approach where learning experiences could include learning labs and peer observations with you. These occurrences should have a directed focus on students in key areas related to the beginning teacher's needs and goal, such as maintaining relationships with students or the use of formative assessment.

An instructional coach can also partner with you and play a helpful role in building collective teacher efficacy within each of the layers of Student-Centered Mentoring. Specifically, participating in a Mentor Coaching Cycle or planning are options to consider for you and your mentee. Chapter 6 is about how you can partner with an instructional coach in the Mentor Coaching Cycle. Planning lessons or activities, with an instructional coach or even another teammate is an informal support where instructional practices are discussed and solutions can be given to mentees. Figure 1.4 summarizes the characteristics of a teacher-centered induction program compared to a student-centered program.

MENTOR TIP

Consider the foundations of a Student-Centered Mentoring approach and brainstorm additional responsibilities or ideas you have to support your mentee(s). Add these ideas to your list from Strategy #2.

Figure 1.4 Comparison of Teacher-Centered Versus Student-Centered Induction Approach

	Teacher-Centered	Student-Centered
Focus	The focus is on the teacher practices.	The focus is on student learning.
Methods	The new teacher(s) are provided with curriculum content and pacing, along with other physical support that fit the necessary guidelines.	A variety of instructional methods are incorporated in delivery of information and how to assess the learning of students, coupled with building collective efficacy beliefs.
Follow-Up	Mentors as well as other building staff may be assigned to meet with and observe new teachers to give feedback on the teacher's effectiveness.	Mentors collaborate regularly with new teachers and observe students during learning activities to assist in setting next steps based on the new teachers' goals, as well as revising them based on student evidence.
Goals	Administrators and mentors assist in setting next steps based on teacher-centered methods.	Administrators and mentors assist in setting next steps based on student learning and teacher clarity.

	Teacher-Centered	Student-Centered
Process	Regularly scheduled induction meetings occur with required informational sessions by the state. Mentor professional development may also be a part of the process.	Regular meetings take place tailored to the needs of the current group of new teachers and their students. Mentor training includes collaborative work sessions with new teachers.
Depth	New teachers may observe other teachers at random, either in the building, district, or other locations.	New teachers and mentors jointly attend learning labs and peer observations that have a directed focus on students in key areas identified as essential for beginning teachers.

ACTION STEP #2: CONNECT THE STUDENT-CENTERED APPROACH TO THE MENTOR FRAMEWORK

Shifting toward a student-centered approach means being more practical in supporting beginning teachers as facilitators of their own classroom of students. It also means being more effective in supporting you, the mentor, as teacher leaders. All of this comes down to growing our impact on students. As Hattie (Hattie, & Zierer, 2018) states, "The narrative in a school should be less about 'how to teach' and more about the 'impact of teaching" (p. 27). Rather than a silo approach to teacher learning and support, the power comes from combining the learning for mentees and mentors through a focus on the students. The layers of Student-Centered Mentoring give you a visual of how to grow your learning and have an impact on students together (Figure 1.5).

Each of the layers eventually meshes together, but you may dive into one layer before another depending on your mentee and their students' needs. There may also be times where you revisit a layer as the mentoring partnership grows. Also, keep your inquiry of beliefs handy. The questions and responses can guide your learning of the Student-Centered Mentoring layers and support growth of your beliefs along the way. An integral part is to think about how you can use the Layers of Student-Centered Mentoring in conjunction with your new understanding of the student-centered philosophy to impact all students, as well as support new teachers.

Figure **1.5** **Layers of Student-Centered Mentoring**

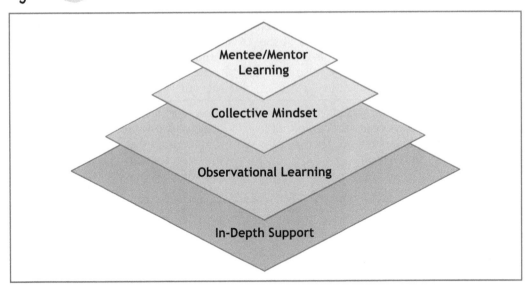

FROM THE LENS OF A NEW TEACHER

How I Started Believing in My Abilities to Impact All Students

I was lucky as a new teacher. I grew up around many teachers and practically lived at school with my relatives. I had confidence in my knowledge of what to expect with planning and grading because I witnessed the process on a regular basis. Despite my background experience, however, I was always questioning how to best help all of my students learn. I focused on engaging students through projects or by the way I delivered my instruction. But my mind always questioned whether I was on the right track or if I should be doing something differently. Here is an experience from my first year of teaching that uncovers a lesson I am glad to have learned:

> It was about midway through my first school year, and I was faced with a dilemma. I arrived at school about an hour and a half early, as I normally did, to prepare for the day. Once there, I received a phone message from one of my fifth-grade students saying she was unable to come to school today. She explained that she had to stay home (for the third day in a row) to babysit

her siblings. At first, my thoughts were centered on her well-being. Who did I need to go to for help? What could I even do for her? Then the academic questions arose. How was she ever going to learn if she was unable to come to school? How could she focus on academics if she was worried about circumstances at home?

It finally made sense to me why she seemed distracted and defensive with other students. After reaching out for advice from a few colleagues, I decided to seek out my administration the following day. We made a plan to immediately implement regular counselor sessions and tutoring support. I also would have a weekly small group lunch with her and a few of her grade-level friends. After a week of being absent, the student finally returned to school, only to get in a fight with another student during P.E. that first day back. That was the final straw for her, and she never returned to our school. My time with her felt abruptly over and to this day, I think about her and wonder if I made any impact on her life.

Despite the sadness I felt from that situation, I walked away learning some big lessons and that I was on the right track—but only because it was pointed out to me by my colleagues. I was seeking assistance. I was asking the right questions. I was putting forth the effort to make a difference with that student. I was told to continue caring. That experience and the feedback changed how I worked with similar students in the future. I may not have fit the mold of every new teacher because of my exposure in my early years, but I knew I had room to grow and wish I had had more of a student-centered philosophy in my beginning years. If you have ever heard the saying, "If only I knew then what I know now," you would probably understand how I could wish for that in my moments with that student. I learned to believe in my connections with students and colleagues.

Not a day goes by that I don't wonder if I could have been more proactive in doing something to help that particular student. Getting to know more about my students' background and understanding more about being responsive to all learners would have given me a clearer view of how to identify her needs. It also would have led me to see some signs sooner. Learning to be confident in myself to make an impact on her despite all other factors in her life was still a substantial takeaway. So how can any new teacher learn to devise a high sense of efficacy—confidence in their ability to affect student learning—in order to impact student learning at a higher and faster rate? Student-Centered Mentoring can help.

(Continued)

(Continued)

MENTOR TIP

Share this Lens of a Mentee experience with your mentee and highlight the lesson learned: Learn to be confident in yourself to make an impact on students despite all other factors in their life.

FROM THE LENS OF A MENTOR

How Diane Grounded Her Mentoring Focus Around Students

Diane is a veteran teacher who, like many others, has mentored many teachers throughout her years in education. Diane has a natural approach and high expectations for her students. She has strong relationships, and students truly enjoy being in her classroom.

When Diane met Tori, she was a brand-new teacher fresh out of college, with less than a year of teaching under her belt. Tori was a passionate and knowledgeable first-year teacher. Here is Diane's reflection about her mentoring experience with Tori:

> Thinking back to that year with Tori, I remember our planning time the most. We made time to discuss the main subjects on a regular basis, resulting in staying after school at a minimum of three days a week for several weeks. To many, that may seem like a great deal of extra time, but I believe it saved us each time in the long run.
>
> Tori and I would collaborate and bounce ideas off each other the most about what in our curriculum resources would best help students learn the skills or content. We talked about what we wanted students to be able to do in the units and how to get them there. Planning was more than just discussing the information of a subject. It was sharing how to engage students in the topic and getting them to practice a skill in varied ways depending on their needs and styles of learning. We looked at student evidence together and talked about what student mastery looked and sounded like.

During one of those conversations, I shared about a time where I thought students nailed their understanding of a concept from a lesson. Sitting at my kitchen table that night, I was upset as I realized after looking over my students' work that a majority of them did not get it at all. I banged my fist on the table and yelled out, "How did they miss this?" As I shared that moment with Tori, it was reassuring for her to see that part of the planning process—reflecting on student work. We helped each other to then decide my next steps. Teaching is hard, it's messy, and can be very frustrating. Students are not always going to learn something the first time. Recognizing when they do and don't, along with how to best teach them, is what planning is really about.

Diane has a student-centered approach in her thinking. Planning to her is more about how to help the students rather than always what to teach in a lesson. The guidance she provided Tori helped Tori to use her time wisely and keep her planning focus on students.

MENTOR TIP

Consider Diane's story to guide you in planning with your mentee. Planning is more about how to help the students rather than always how to teach a lesson.

RECAP AND REFLECT

A student-centered approach is an effective structure to use with new teachers and can be balanced with a teacher-centered approach. In order to retain teachers and make the most impact on students, we have to begin to layer in the characteristics of a student-centered mindset when working with new teachers. Figure 1.6 shows how key features of a student-centered approach can be incorporated into the layers of Student-Centered Mentoring for new teachers. By doing this, you can increase efficacious beliefs for new teachers and promote a meaningful partnership while increasing the impact on student learning. From administrators and district officials to mentors and coaches, all of those involved in training new teachers are vital in the process. Whether you are starting from scratch or have mentored before, you are in the right place to obtain new ideas to support mentees in their beginning years.

Figure **1.6** Layers of Student-Centered Mentoring with Key Ideas

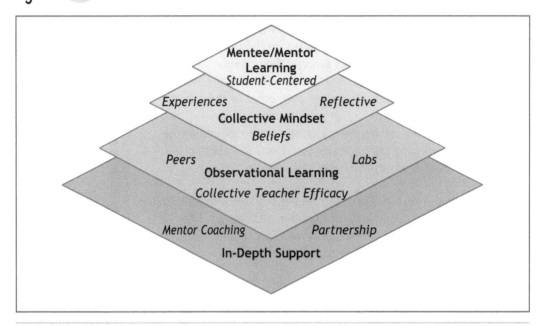

MENTOR INQUIRY REFLECTION

Reflect on the questions that follow. Use the Rubric for Student-Centered Mentoring Section #1 to help set goals and make a plan for yourself (Figure 1.7).

1. What is the current state of new teacher induction in your school or district?

2. How would you define Student-Centered Mentoring?

3. In what areas can you shift your mentoring moves to embrace a more student-centered approach?

4. Which Student-Centered Mentoring success criteria would you choose to support this shift?

5. What are some initial action steps you can take to achieve a more student-centered approach?

Fיgure **1.7** Rubric for Student-Centered Mentoring

#1: Understand the Student-Centered Mentoring Approach and Practice the Strategies With Mentees		
Beginner	**Emerging**	**Innovative**
The mentor is accepting of the role of a mentor and is willing to learn Student-Centered Mentor strategies. He/She has yet to attempt any of the student-centered practices.	The mentor is attempting to learn skills and techniques that are student centered as well as trying a portion of a Student-Centered Mentoring component (i.e., philosophy, framework, strategies, etc.).	The mentor shares in the Student-Centered Mentoring belief system and empowers others to consider similar thoughts. He/She takes a lead role in employing the strategies within his/her daily practices and school as well as seeks opportunities to build the student-centered knowledge of other educators.

Success Criteria

- I can build a set of student-centered beliefs in partnership with my mentee.

- I can apply Student-Centered Mentoring strategies within the mentoring experience.

- I can connect the mentor partnership goals to current school/district goals.

- I can celebrate the easy and difficult steps in using effective instructional and mentoring practices, keeping the focus on student learning.

- I can arrange opportunities for us to observe student learning centered on my mentee's goals.

- I can seek ways to gain varied support for my mentee from other school/district staff members.

LAYING THE FOUNDATION FOR A STRONG MENTORING RELATIONSHIP

A mentoring partnership involves working together to fully guide new teachers through their beginning years. Laying a foundation from the start leads to supporting mentees instructionally, emotionally, physically, and conversationally. There will be times when the best laid plans may go awry and you may have to answer impromptu questions or give advice at any given moment. For instance, I walked into Lauren's room for our planning time on what I thought was a normal day after school and immediately knew something was off. From that moment, I could tell she was frustrated. I honestly didn't know if I should stay for our scheduled meeting or turn around and walk out. I knew Lauren was not upset at me, but she was at her breaking point. How many of us have been in a similar situation, where we walk into another teacher's classroom during a break or after school and instantly recognize that what we were planning to do or discuss or work on needed to be put on hold. Truthfully, it was clear that my next step was to help Lauren work through something difficult. She explained that her breaking point was earlier in the day when she had to make her first student office referral. Lauren was extremely upset and somewhat disheartened as well. I tried to reassure her that she was not a horrible teacher for needing to use that form of behavior management, gave her several suggestions for handling related experiences, and even shared a similar event from my first year teaching. Unfortunately, I don't think I responded in the way she needed, judging by the sad look on Lauren's face. I gave her too much information all at once, which ended up making her feel even more frustrated and overwhelmed. Do I wish I had had some professional learning on how to be more of a listener and ask questions in the moment? Of course!

As a mentor, you are an important piece of the puzzle in supporting, training, and retaining new teachers. But it is also vital for mentors to receive training and support as you guide novice teachers. Think back to the layers of Student-Centered Mentoring (Figure 2.1); the top layer includes mentor learning. Maintaining a cycle of appropriate and effective support is important for both mentees as well as mentors. Whether you are a fellow teacher, an instructional coach, or even an administrator, as a mentor you will benefit from some professional learning support so you can learn how to best approach student-centered conversations with mentees. This book will equip you to lead these conversations, which are crucial to improving student learning and developing new teachers' skills and confidence.

Figure 2.1 Layers of Student-Centered Mentoring With Key Ideas

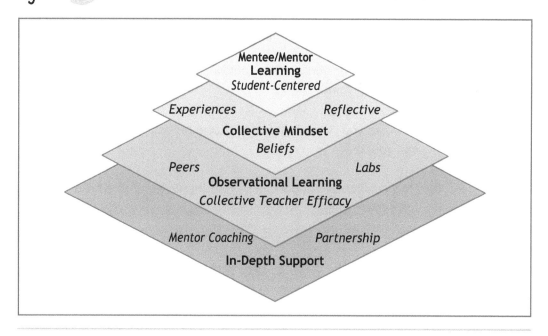

WHAT IS THIS CHAPTER ABOUT?

In this chapter, you will learn strategies to

> Support positive emotions with new teachers

> Build strong mentoring relationships with a focus on students

> Provide effective feedback to your mentee and to students

A large part of a mentor's role in the mentoring partnership is listening to the needs of new teachers and their students and then forming relevant feedback. It starts by building a relationship with your mentee. It is also helpful to remind yourself of your own beginning experiences as you shift to a student-centered planning routine and boost your professional learning in these areas. In this chapter, we will uncover directional supports that promote a positive and supportive mentoring partnership and guide the differentiation that mentees need to be successful.

MENTOR INQUIRY PRE-REFLECTION

Use these guiding questions as you explore the ideas in this chapter:

1. What areas do you want to consider as you begin your mentoring work?

2. How can you promote positive thoughts with students, colleagues, and yourself?

3. How can you be supportive of your mentee and give feedback at the same time?

THE IMPORTANCE OF A POSITIVE AND SUPPORTIVE PARTNERSHIP

Mentor programs and evaluation tools have one thing in common, and that is they begin by building relationships with students. Starting a mentoring partnership in a similar way is supportive of a mentee's overall well-being and success as a teacher. First and foremost, human connection is vital to the mentor relationship. Dr. Carrington (2019) shares in her book, *Kids These Days*, that with all relationships, it all comes down to "connection." Her thinking is in line with the philosophy behind Student-Centered Mentoring. Also imperative to our work when teaching gets tough is connections with others. Mentor relationships are important in dealing with stress, especially beginning teacher stress, which we will go further into during Chapter 3.

Angela Caves is a mentor at Prairie View Middle School in Brighton, Colorado, and attended a Student-Centered Mentoring session that focused on relationship work first. Her takeaway was that building relationships with colleagues the same way that she currently builds relationships with students can be extremely powerful in new teacher partnerships (personal communication, January 14, 2021). She shared as a follow-up to that work that staying present and working to understand both student and mentee needs is key. She adds that those steps support the relationship connection needed for progress to be made. The mentor relationships then underpin effectively collaborating with mentees.

With any partnership, we have to begin with getting to know the other person. But a true working relationship is built on trust and openness. How do we make that happen with our mentees? It starts with positivity. How do we then guide beginning teachers to be successful? Our attention then has to be directed toward students as the main topic, in order to make the most impact in a mentee's classroom of learners. All of this leads to a key component of a strong foundation—feedback.

As humans, we crave feedback. Whether we are open to the actual feedback itself depends on many characteristics for both the giving and receiving of the information. Considering the innovator mindset I have, I always enjoy learning something new from colleagues. I also like to hear what I am specifically doing well at, especially from those who I look up to. Therefore, I am open to hearing suggestions of what I can do to continue growing in my craft. I have not always been in that state though. As I reflect on how I made it to this point and couple that with what I learned from other new teachers and mentors, I have noticed that a positive relationship has to be built together first before giving feedback. Let's take Andrea and Katie's mentor partnership for example. Andrea, Katie's mentor, appreciates collaboration with her teammates and models reflective thinking with students regularly. During Katie's first several months, I also noticed that Andrea promoted time to eat lunch together with Katie daily and check in on her regularly.

MENTOR TIP

Set up a regular check-in meeting with mentees and be on the lookout for professional learning that helps you both in continuing to grow and strengthen your partnership.

LEADING YOUR MENTEE IN THE RIGHT DIRECTION

As you uncover your mentee's needs for support, you will want to categorize the types of support into four categories. It can best be explained in a directional nature, as we can all use the help of a compass when we are lost. Utilize the directional supports to showcase emotional, physical, communication, and instructional support (Figure 2.2). A strong mentoring partnership attends to all four directions at some point. There are moments in a journey that we need to begin our track in a certain direction and then change directions as a path is adjusted. The same can be said for starting in a specific direction to assist mentees—based on their individual and student needs.

Figure 2.2   Directional Supports

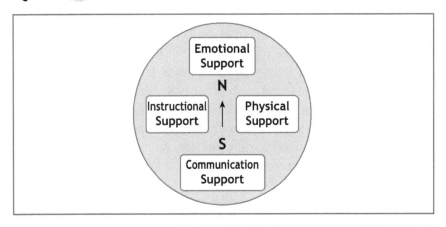

Just as having the internal awareness of north helps us to find our way, especially when lost, having emotional support as north on a compass reiterates the importance of emotional well-being always being in the forefront of our minds. At times, you may need to change the direction of your path and give the support needed in one of the other categories. Communication is a key piece in supporting conversations with others, especially students. You cannot forget the physical needs that can include informational tips or even where to find places in the school. Last but not least is instructional support. This is where the rubber meets the road and supports the instructional methods taught to students. Have you noticed a trend as to what can initiate a strong mentoring partnership? Support! Support in a student-centered focus toward meeting the needs of your mentee is most evident.

Figure 2.3 Summary of Directional Supports

Emotional	Communication	Physical	Instructional
Your North!	*Your South!*	*Your East!*	*Your West!*
Emotional support encompasses the health and well-being of teachers and students.	Communication support pertains to the interactions from student-to-student, student-to-teacher, teacher-to-colleague, and teacher-to-parent.	Physical support involves tangible and procedural parts that are accustomed to the role of teaching.	Instructional support entails the use of teaching practices centered on methods and instructional strategies.
It includes	It includes	It includes	It includes
• Knowing and understanding the trauma students face • Social-emotional needs of both students and teachers themselves • Absence of self-care of a teacher	• Student management concerns • Parent phone calls • Collaboration norms with teammates • Observations from administrators	• Providing information about locations • Figuring out copiers or other building resources • Building procedures and schedules • Classroom setup	• Choosing appropriate methods and instructional strategies to meet student needs • Observing job-alike classrooms to deepen the instructional impact of students • Discussing impact on student learning and achievement

Adapted from Boogren (2015)

MENTOR TIP

Use Appendix G, the Digital Companion Resource: Directional Supports for Beginning Teachers Handout to have as an at-a-glance document. Also, share the resource with your mentee as it summarizes the four areas and can be a guide for conversations.

STRATEGIES FOR SETTING UP AN EFFECTIVE MENTORING PARTNERSHIP

Your role as a mentor will more than likely continue into your mentee's second and third year of teaching. Possibly even longer! As a mentor, you are not only integral within the layers of Student-Centered Mentoring for new teachers, but your relationship will be a safe haven for your mentee. Both of you will grow in your craft, and that results in the growth of even more students. In order for these benefits to occur, it takes some time to lay the groundwork for a mutual and trusting relationship. A supportive relationship will lead you to being able to give the feedback necessary for growth. Throughout this chapter, you will gain insight on strategies that will provide your mentoring partnership a start toward a positive relationship and add to your mentoring toolbox. Strategies 2 and 5 will give you multiple action steps to assist in the process.

STRATEGY #1: SHARE YOUR PERSONAL EXPERIENCES

Think back to when you were a beginning teacher and the experiences that molded your early years. Most of us remember our first evaluation—the nerves and the intrinsic desire for it to go well. My first observation was scheduled during a reading lesson, and I thought it was a disaster. The administrator was running behind, so I waited to start. Of course, the students were a little bit antsy by the time she arrived, and I was right there with them. We finally got started, and I wasn't even a minute in when a student threw up on the carpet— luckily not on anyone else. I quickly got the students settled back in their seats, called the custodian, and continued to teach my lesson. The custodian was as fast as ever in responding to the call. I kept on teaching, even though students were trying not to gag at the smell. Afterward, I felt defeated as I shared my experience of turmoil with my mentor and teammates. Their responses were reassuring: "You kept teaching?" and "Your students will actually remember more than you think." To my surprise, the students did remember some things. I also received good ratings on my evaluation because of my persistence in teaching the lesson! This experience was yet another early lesson for me that the way students respond is far more important than having a "perfect" lesson.

There are other moments you may recall more vividly than others. What memory seems to stick with you forever? Also, think about the experiences that are more general that could help you share a pearl of wisdom. Consider this list as you recall both positive and negative memories:

- First office referral
- Field trips
- Classroom interruptions
- Parent-teacher conferences
- Unexpected student responses

Any of these moments can be disheartening no matter how smoothly the process plays out. I will never forget dealing with harassment from a student and how it took a toll on me, as it would any teacher. I couldn't believe my ears heard it correctly when a student was making inappropriate comments to another student. Then, I found out they also had said things in reference to me as well. The piece that has risen to the surface as I go down memory lane is that all teachers can experience these impressionable moments, causing an emotional toll that shapes us into who we are as educators. As a mentor, it is important for us to think back to those experiences that molded us in our beginning years. When we share what was learned from those moments, it helps us relate to our mentees and builds a sense of trust and mutual respect.

MENTOR TIP

If your memory is a little fuzzy recalling other experiences, try asking yourself, What situations have made me nervous? When have I felt really disheartened? What has excited me? When did I see the light bulb moment for a student? You might even look at class pictures or yearbooks. Just remember to share some of those moments and what you learned from them with your mentee.

STRATEGY #2: SUPPORT POSITIVE EMOTIONS WITH NEW TEACHERS

We know from experience that being a new teacher can feel uncertain at times, which is why it is so important to guide mentees with positive support. Whether trying to find a sense of direction as a mentee or even as a mentor, teaching can take an emotional toll. You will want to use these action steps to help you steer your mentee in a hopeful direction as well as to grow your mentoring relationship through optimism.

ACTION STEP #1: PROMOTE A POSITIVE OUTLOOK

For a new teacher, it is easy to feel like you are frantically running around in circles with no sense of direction making little progress with students. As mentors, to help remove those feelings of chaos, we must encourage a positive frame of mind. One easy way to do this is to start the day with positive affirmations that it is going to be a good day. More than likely, the positive thinking will promote an easier day or at least make the challenges that arise easier to deal with. As humans, we have to intentionally work to think on the bright side. We tend to let negative experiences play a toll on ourselves more than we allow positivity, which shapes our relationships. As VeryWellMind states from a compilation of research, "The negative bias is our tendency not only to register negative stimuli more readily but also to dwell on these events (Cherry, 2020). Overcoming this requires retraining our daily outlooks and promoting a positive outlook. I remember recommending this with my grandmother right after she had a severe heart attack and was in ICU. We started a notebook and I encouraged her to think of three things she was thankful for each day. It helped her. She progressed and gained enough strength to eventually go home.

MENTOR TIP

Advocate for positive thinking to help your mentee have a more optimistic outlook about each day. Reiterate that it will make the issues that arise easier to deal with as well.

Some of the teachers I work with regularly will also tell you that I encourage a similar thought process. We even sometimes text each other what we are thankful for when we know it is going to be a more challenging day. How does this all connect to the daily job of being a teacher? If we can remind ourselves of the joys of teaching, then a natural by-product is the hope of making a difference with our students. Being a model of positive thinking for our students creates the domino effect for our students' to then learn.

Another aspect is how we feel others perceive our actions. "People often fear the consequences of the negative outcome more than they desire the potential positive gains, even when the two possibilities are equivalent" says Cherry (2020). As a teacher, we can feel judged for teaching a specific strategy over another or for how we talk with a student about their work, to name just a few. That is because of the possibility of it not working or being incorrect. You have the opportunity to help your mentee promote the positive possibilities instead. This will help diffuse some of the negative self-doubt and establish a happier relationship for you both.

ACTION STEP #2: GUIDE YOUR MENTEE NORTH WITH THE DIRECTIONAL SUPPORTS

Imagine walking around a forest with no sense of direction like Dorothy in *The Wizard of Oz*. She needed the encouragement and positive support to find her way to the Emerald City. Mentors and mentees think similarly as Dorothy. Many ask, "How do we know if we are on the right path?" "How do we know if our choices are effective?" One thing I believe deep down will help educators find the pathway out of this forest and make an impact on students' learning is to support each other by keeping a focus on the north. What does that really mean though? To get out of a forest, whether with someone or alone, one of the first steps is to get your sense of direction. Focus on looking for the moss on trees. Moss only grows on the north side, so you can use that knowledge to help keep from circling back to where you started.

The start of getting out of the forest is positive thinking, which is an integral piece of the emotional direction. Think back to Katie earlier in this chapter. Katie is very reflective of her own practices and sometimes feels as though she could be doing more for her students. Knowing her passion, Andrea instilled the importance of certain routine practices that contributed to her emotional well-being. This allowed them to move in another direction when needed. Andrea encouraged emotional well-being support along with instructional support. How did Andrea know to do this? In part, she knew based on information that was provided to her during a mentor professional learning session that covered how to support beginning teachers. But the main reason is her intrinsic nature to lead Katie in the direction she needed most. Think of ways to encourage the positive emotional well-being of mentees so they can have a sense of direction with their students. Now that we have a sense of our north, we will explore the other supports in further sections of this chapter: communication, physical, and instructional.

MENTOR TIP

Start with the directional support of north to guide your mentee toward positive emotions and set the stage for next steps of support. You will also need to shift north from time to time, sometimes on a whim.

STRATEGY #3: ASK QUESTIONS TO DETERMINE APPROPRIATE SUPPORT

Having effective conversations with mentees includes questioning. By asking specific questions up front, you can save time and frustration, as well as learn about your mentee. Questioning can also clarify the types of support your mentee needs. You will want to reflect on how to be an effective communicator and then eventually it will become routine to ask questions. Embedding more questions into dialogue also allows mentees to share their thinking first. Your mentee could even solve their own problems! If we, as mentors, go right into replying when we are approached with a problem, beginning teachers are less likely to feel heard, as well as learn. Communication is vital in building an effective relationship with any individual. Trusting partnerships are not only based on honesty but open conversations as well. So when needed, turn the compass south and encourage talking it out.

IN THE CLASSROOM

Questioning promotes dialogue. This same questioning approach can be used to encourage dialogue with students. Help students understand the purpose of asking questions is to understand each other and encourage deeper questions in partnerships or small groups to increase learning. Invite your mentee to brainstorm together some open-ended questions to model the start of the process for students.

Let's revisit the directional supports and consider what questions to ask mentees in order to discover the possible support that is needed. Does your mentee need help with physical needs, like arranging their classroom to promote partnership and group work? What about instructional needs, like how to teach a specific reading strategy to a higher-level group of students? Or is it emotional needs, like struggling with how to help a student who is experiencing trauma? If we really want to provide the appropriate support, then clarifying the state teachers are in will help the next steps of the partnership. The intentional questions asked can also tie to giving useful feedback when needed and guiding next steps. If you are uncertain of the specific directional questions to ask, consider a more general approach that embeds a student-centered focus. This will also help your mentee feel less judged for their actions and open to suggestions, as well as support positivity. Some guiding questions that mentors can ask of themselves are the following:

- What kind of questions are you asking your mentee in relation to the student outcomes?

- Are you asking surface-level questions or going more in depth?

- How are mentees themselves asking questions in relation to students?

- What do the majority of your mentee's students experience when outside of school that could affect their day-to-day well-being?

KEEPING IT STUDENT CENTERED

It tends to be more natural to ask mentees the physical questions of support, like whether they know how to use the copier. Try to adapt your questioning to be focused more around students. Ask yourself the guiding questions as you try to be more student centered. It can help when talking with your mentee and take the judgmental nature out of the conversation that some mentees may feel. Also, just like with students, mentees are then better able to solve their own problems.

STRATEGY #4: BALANCE PLANNING CONVERSATIONS TO INCLUDE STUDENTS AND CONTENT

Normally, the assumption is that new teachers need mostly content support, which is why many induction programs include a heavy emphasis on this area. This represents a teacher-centered viewpoint where the focus is on creating the expert teacher. But information changes quickly in our world and factual knowledge is at the tip of our fingers. So having the focus so much on content decreases the importance of the students in front of us. "What do I teach my students?" is a common question and can still be a part of the planning. However, you can reframe this question to be, "How do I teach the learners?" instead. By doing this, we can help teachers keep their passion for learning about their craft alive and keep the heart of why we are in the profession up front—our students.

MENTOR TIP

Start all of your planning conversations by looking at student evidence and asking about student observations. If you plan together weekly or even daily, try having the first 10 minutes always encompass student work.

As a mentor, how do you balance that planning to include students and learning strategies that will be most impactful? The idea is to increase talk about students and student evidence. It is extremely helpful to mentors who are not in the same content area as their mentee to plan strategic questions for use in planning conversations. This will allow you to have a student-centered focus and assist in planning quality instruction. Rodney, a mentor in an elementary school outside of St. Louis, shared that a big takeaway for him was incorporating how to discuss and celebrate the growth of students with his mentee. "When we have these conversations together, we can celebrate each other. It helps us to learn about each other's strengths as teachers and share ways to help each other and our students." Some planning questions that can guide planning conversations with a student-centered focus are the following:

▶ What student work can we look at to guide next steps?

▶ How are the students showing you their learning?

▶ What do the majority of your students already know?

▶ How can we keep students engaged?

▶ Why do we want the students to learn this information?

▶ What instructional strategies match the students' needs at this time?

STRATEGY #5: PROVIDE EFFECTIVE FEEDBACK TO YOUR MENTEE

One of the top-rated strategies in the mentor ranking of professional learning is mentors giving feedback to their mentee. Giving effective feedback is more than just a comment in response to an action. It begins with active and supportive listening. The feedback process then includes understanding of both giving and receiving feedback. This high impact strategy is then best utilized by forming strengths-based feedback, where you center the feedback around strengths and skills. The feedback loop comes full circle as you continually go through the process and layer feedback that relates to recent feedback, helping your mentee make connections from one experience to the next. Use these action steps to reinforce a positive relationship with your mentee.

ACTION STEP #1: MODEL ACTIVE LISTENING

After asking clarifying questions, mentors need to truly listen to the responses before providing feedback. There is power in listening. Just like finding a sense of direction in the forest, listening to what's going on around you is important. In conversation, it is second nature to think in the moment about what we would do in a situation and reply immediately. Instead, we should be listening to understand.

In his book *We Got This*, Minor (2019) describes listening in three phases. First is the act of listening itself—more specifically, hearing. Second, we have some thinking to process what we heard and seek to understand. Finally, based on what is heard, we then ask questions. How do I make revisions to my teaching and my classroom community? How do I adjust to how everything around me operates? How do we listen to understand what students are communicating? So I think of these parts for listening in three easy steps: hear, think, and ask.

Beginning teachers need mentors and colleagues who will listen to their needs. As a mentor, we have to listen to mentees first in order to know what kind of support to give them. Whether it is more physical support, such as how to use the new LMS (learning management system), or further supporting emotional needs, we cannot make assumptions; we must listen. And in all reality, the same goes for any of our colleagues.

This small action of listening can be helpful, especially after teaching students to be assessment-capable learners. John Hattie's work around developing assessment-capable learners could be a great direction to help guide you on that right path of listening to students and their learning. It is powerful to use student evidence as you listen to students, as well as brainstorm ways to promote better listening with students. Try it yourself and then share the experience with your mentee so they can listen to students as well! Here are two sets of questions to use as you collaborate with your mentee about the act of listening:

What evidence can we use to be more intuitive with students?

- Student survey data

- Student achievement data

- Student observations

- Interviews or conversations

How do we promote being better listeners with students?

- Class meeting discussions

- Book clubs

- Group work

- Partner reading

- Providing examples of listening characteristics

- Modeling being a listener during presentations

 IN THE CLASSROOM

The same listening process—hear, think, ask—can be used with students as well (Minor, 2019). Just like with mentees, the assumption cannot be made as to what students' needs may be unless we listen. As a mentor, start off with listening to your students and their needs. This could be listening to what and how they say things. It also includes listening to their learning and understanding what they may be struggling with.

Additionally, I invite you to take the challenge of listening to your own listening. Since technology is readily available, you can easily do that by watching a recording from an activity with your class. You could also ask colleagues to record one of your planning sessions. If you're unable to record any of those opportunities, just thinking and being mindful of how you listen is a powerful follow-up reflection. Consider times of interruptions, pauses, and even your body language when you are trying to be two steps ahead in the conversation. Lastly, don't be afraid to ask more questions!

MENTOR TIP

Be a model of listening to understand with teammates, staff, and students. Promote the challenge of listening to your own listening. My favorite is videoing a small group or conference with a student!

ACTION STEP #2: BE GIVERS AND RECEIVERS OF FEEDBACK

Now we are ready for what many think of as the most important strategy of a mentor's role: delivering feedback. Before delving into how to give feedback to mentees, it is important to explore several aspects—mentor concerns and the characteristics of being a receiver as well as giver of feedback. This is where a relationship with mentees can go awry. It is also the aspect of mentoring that many mentors feel unsure about. One mentor shared that it sometimes intimidates her to give feedback, but learning how to keep the feedback based on strengths and using a process makes it feel less intimidating and something she feels more comfortable doing the more she does it (Sherry, personal communication, January 11, 2021). So let's dive into the other parts of that process for you to be prepared as well!

It is important to consider the characteristics of feedback and expectations within the mentoring partnership. This is especially true for the attributes of both giving and receiving effective feedback (see Figure 2.4). Even though most of the characteristics are applicable to both the giver and receiver, you will notice the majority lie with the receiver. This is where we have to consider not only learning how to give feedback but also how to receive it. In *Thanks for the Feedback,* Stone and Heen (2014) describe how giving feedback skillfully only goes so far if the receiver is unwilling or unable to absorb the information. Helping mentees be engaged receivers of feedback is the key to unlock learning. So instead of pushing, we instill pulling.

Creating pull is about mastering the skills required to drive our own learning; it's about how to recognize and manage our resistance, how to engage in feedback conversations with confidence and curiosity, and even when the feedback goes wrong, how to find insight that might help us grow. It's also about how to stand up for who we are and how we see the world and ask for what we need. (Stone & Heen, 2014, p. 6)

Figure 2.4 Characteristics of Giving and Receiving Feedback

Characteristic	Giver	Receiver
Coach	✓	
Role model	✓	
Open to ideas		✓
Reflective		✓
Seeks relevance		✓
Choices		✓
Listener	✓	✓
Collaborator	✓	✓
Seeks growth	✓	✓
Positive	✓	✓
Innovator	✓	✓
Problem solver	✓	✓

The top of the list for both givers and receivers includes listening, covered earlier in the chapter. Listening is not only valuable in a relationship but also when incorporated into the feedback loop. Another characteristic to point out is from the receiver side of seeking relevance. As a receiver, truly feeling as though tips and suggestions are relevant feels personal. Several other characteristics for the receiver—growth, innovator, open to ideas, reflective, and problem solver—fall under having a learning mindset, which we will cover more in depth in Chapter 3. An important area to also keep in mind for a receiver is having a choice of next steps. As humans, we tend to work well when given a few options. It is noticeable in a strong mentoring partnership how mentees respond well to being given choice.

MENTOR TIP

Helping mentees to become receivers of feedback is the key to unlock learning. Show the chart to your mentee and analyze characteristics of giving and receiving feedback together to help support the feedback process.

As mentors, it is also important to consider the categories of feedback in the mentoring partnership (see Figure 2.5). As you examine the categories, you will also notice qualities of giving effective feedback are embedded throughout. The first two categories—promote and praise—are where the effective feedback characteristics are most evident. Promote tops the list because that is where the mentoring partnership will be the most student centered as well as make the most impact. It is where you will collaborate and generate ideas about student learning. Praise is meant to be celebratory of results and increase motivation. To persuade is to be more teacher centered in the feedback approach, where you will inform your mentee about specific details around concepts and moments. There may be rare occasions the directness may be needed, so keep in mind how to shift to using the other feedback categories. The same can be said for the perceive category. This can be more related to the evaluation of mentees but solely recommended for the administrator to do.

Figure 2.5 Categories of Feedback in a Mentoring Partnership

	Characterized by	Purpose
Promote	• Listening, questioning, paraphrasing, probing, withholding judgment • Mutual brainstorming, clarifying, deciding, assessing impact on students	• Coach and collaborator • Student-centered decision making (what students currently understand and can do) and promote ongoing reflection in order to expand/ sharpen knowledge, skills, and capability • Generate ideas to solve instructional problems, apply and test shared ideas, and learn together through co-planning
Praise	• Recognition, encouragement, gratitude	• Increase motivation • Acknowledge results, hard work, and effort in order to motivate and thank

(Continued)

	Characterized by	Purpose
Persuade	• Directness • Giving advice or suggestions • Modeling and demonstrating	• Inform about details regarding policies, procedures, content, techniques, and events
Perceive	• Observing actions • Judging • Commenting • Measuring	• Evaluate progress and results for significance • Performance-based in the moment

ACTION STEP #3: USE STRENGTHS-BASED FEEDBACK

Finally, we get to the *"how"* of providing feedback. The strengths-based feedback approach falls in the promote and praise category of feedback. I first heard of giving strengths-based feedback when I began my role as a coach. I learned to use a three-step process with Sweeney (Sweeney & Harris, 2017). This is one approach you could take with your mentee. The three steps are as follows:

1. **Clarify:** Ask clarifying questions and probe to learn more about details, successes, and difficulties

2. **Value:** Celebrate what is working and showcase strengths and actions

3. **Uncover possibilities:** Devise a goal and define next step(s)

Let's compare that to the sandwich approach. Most know this method as an area of need shared between two positive comments, not necessarily about the same focus. Well, I may still use that at times, like with my husband, but there is another option to keep in mind. I have since formed a technique using some of the strengths-based feedback parts but in a two-step process (Figure 2.6). I simplified the process because I found that most mentors and mentees know each other on a more in-depth level. Plus, more than likely questions have already been asked in some way prior to giving feedback. With that in mind, a mentor rarely needs the clarification step before recognizing and brainstorming ideas. More often than not, clarification is blended into the brainstorm phase.

Figure 2.6 Two-Step Process for Strengths-Based Feedback With Mentees

Using Strengths-Based Feedback With Mentees		
	Description	**Language Stems**
1. Recognize	• Builds on the strengths and skills of the mentee with a focus on students • Encourages and recognizes hard work and effort in order to motivate and thank	• How do you plan to . . . ? • The students really responded to . . . • Did you notice how the students engaged in . . . ? • The . . . practice was really effective when . . . • What strategies will you use? • What will success look like? • You really thought about . . . • How will you monitor students' . . . ? • I see how you've been working diligently on . . . • So you're feeling . . . thinking . . .
2. Brainstorm	• Co-constructs ideas to increase mentees' knowledge, skills, and capability focused around understanding and helping students • Promotes ongoing reflection that includes choices and open-ended questions for mentees to consider	• What student evidence leads you to these decisions? • How would you revise . . . ? • How is this compared to how you thought it would be . . . ? • What are some ideas that you have? • What are the causes for . . . ?

The first step is recognizing. This step is about a specific skill or action that is relevant in the moment. The recognition step is one of the most important because it sets the stage for the mentee to think positively. Plus, mentees need to know what they are doing well so that they can continue that practice. More than anything, it helps them keep an open mind to new suggestions or ideas. It is also important to use language that is focused around students. The language stems in Figure 2.6 provide lots of examples to model this. The second step is brainstorming. It includes collaborating around ideas based on the recognition. As a mentor, you are essentially coaching your mentee in a student-centered manner by modeling how to reflect on ideas and process decision making that will benefit students the most. This is when many mentors will use clarifying questions as the co-construction of ideas and next steps propels the collaboration forward.

KEEPING IT STUDENT CENTERED

Giving feedback to mentees and colleagues can be intimidating, especially if you have received a negative response in the past. If you recall giving feedback before, analyze your approach. Then, consider practicing the use of strengths-based feedback language with a focus on the students to make the student-centered wording more of a habit.

Giving feedback using this process with a student-centered focus supports a beginning teacher in making amazing growth with students. Rather than just giving advice or saying, "Good job," you will have more of an effect when being specific and relevant to the skills and instructional practices. Kimberly Warne (personal communication, January 14, 2021), a mentor at Prairie View Middle School in Brighton, Colorado, shared how this approach gives her the opportunity to give feedback to her mentee that is less intimidating and more focused. "It allows me to be able to express the feedback in terms of the student needs and reactions so that the teacher does not feel attacked and can get behind doing whatever is needed for our students!" When you couple strengths-based feedback with guiding mentees toward becoming open receivers of feedback, it makes the feedback loop come full circle. When it comes to achieving the feedback loop, build off past feedback by slowly adding onto suggestions or ideas based on the strengths of your mentee.

IN THE CLASSROOM

This feedback process can be used with students in the classroom as well. Teaching kids to give and receive strengths-based feedback can be embedded into a beginning teacher's daily routine, which promotes a culture of community and learning. This process can be followed when responding to students verbally and in written comments as well. To do this, take some of the stems above and try adapting them to use with students. For example, "I see how you have been working diligently on your use of algebraic expressions. What are some ideas for showing your thinking as you find the answers?"

FROM THE LENS OF A NEW TEACHER

How Lindsay Found Value in Mentoring as a Reentry Teacher

Although she taught for six years, Lindsay was brand new to her district and knew she was in for a learning curve. Lindsay took a first grade position after having previously taught fifth grade, and even though she looked forward to her new position, she had some slight apprehension. She truly did not realize it would be like she was starting over from scratch until after the fact. Luckily, Teena was her buddy mentor and the pair was a perfect match. Here is Lindsay's account of their experience:

The most beneficial part of my work with Teena was the ongoing support and collaboration. We were constantly talking about what worked, what went well with the students, and making plans to adjust where needed. I had to be honest with myself to admit that even though I had been a teacher for six years prior to coming to Heritage, I had VERY little experience with primary grades, and I needed support with reading strategies to help my kids. I am so grateful that I was able to have Teena as a mentor because she was so understanding and supportive.

Specifically, that was a big year for us to learn about how to make a small group reading method we called massive practice (introducing several books, some created together, across a 3-5 day succession with a group). It was successful, and so I think because of having that time to collaborate together and make adjustments to the method is something I'll always remember. Teena helped by listening and giving me encouragement along the way, which made me feel much more confident in the primary level of teaching reading! She was previously a reading interventionist, so her level of knowledge in reading was extremely helpful as I learned the best strategies to teach my first graders.

Being able to try something together makes it a little less scary, and you have someone to talk to along the way. Teena and I even went through a mentor coaching cycle together as well. Because I had her as a supportive mentor, I made quick gains with some of my most struggling readers. Teena also pushed me to be a

(Continued)

(Continued)

risk-taker and really held me accountable for making a plan. It helped me to be intentional with what I was going to do to help my students. If I hadn't gone through that process, I don't think I would have made the increase in effectiveness that I did.

Lindsay highlighted the importance of having Teena's support through her first year in a new grade level and new school. Their mentoring partnership showcased the value of a mentor's listening and guidance in the appropriate direction. Lindsay also mentioned their work in a mentor cycle, which you can read more about in Chapter 6. Teena's participation also made an immense impact on Lindsay's beliefs in herself. The two of them continue to work at the same grade level and refine their teaching practices together to better their students.

FROM THE LENS OF A MENTOR

How Kala Embodied Listening as a Mentor

Kala was a mentor during her sixth year of teaching. She began her teaching career in the same district she is still in today. She also had a wonderful role model to look up to, as her mother was an elementary teacher as well. Kala's mentee, Hannah, had graduated the December before, and that spring semester, she was a building substitute prior to being hired on Kala's team. Kala and Hannah taught on a grade level with three other teachers as well. Kala shared her account of her mentoring partnership with Hannah:

Thinking back to Hannah's interview, I remember that she had hardly left the room when our team announced simultaneously that she was the one we recommended. Hannah was, we could tell, a hard worker and just so eager to get into the classroom. Her enthusiasm was contagious and she worked (and continues to work) so hard. I think that my mentee and I had a very strong relationship because we shared these similar characteristics. We had an immediate connection from the interview and quickly felt lost if we were not talking on a daily basis. We became friends first and colleagues second. Therefore, all our conversations were ones where we assumed the best in each other.

Her first year she had a VERY difficult group of kids, but she never gave up. I have so many memories of Hannah coming to my room, laying across the front carpet, and sprawling out over student desktops to talk. We just knew we could laugh together, sometimes even cry, about whatever issue had come up.

She built a classroom community where everyone felt included and valued. I will never forget the many conversations before, during, and after the school day, even some nights and weekends!

I think the biggest thing is just being there to listen. Being a first-year teacher is HARD! You need to have someone that you know will support you, have your back, give ideas when they are looking for them, and know that they are not being judged in the process. We all go through starting off as a first year teacher and come out on the other side knowing so much more about ourselves. But, we need someone there for us to make sure we don't fall. When my mentee would doubt herself, I would ask why she did it the way she did. Her response usually was because this student or that student needed a basic need met, whether learning or emotional. I then told her that she did it for the kid, to give them what they need. That is what a teacher does and no one would find fault in that. The look of relaxation would hit her and I knew it was the right move at that time.

Now, we are excited to have even moved up to a new grade level, together. Another teacher who had been on the original team that hired Hannah also joined us. It felt like a wonderful reunion that we were all together again! Hannah is a great teacher and coworker, but an even better friend. She attends birthday parties for my boys and I was at her wedding this past fall. She is an amazing person and I am so thankful that I took a "risk" on mentoring a teacher new to the profession.

Kala's takeaway about listening helped her to understand her mentee's needs, along with being someone to confide in. The simple replies centered around meeting the necessities of students helped give her mentee confidence in those moments and encouraged room for more professional learning together. The two of them moved into the other layers of Student-Centered Mentoring, specifically "labs and observations," that is the focus of Chapter 5. The partner learning lab experience was helpful for Kala to add on to her mentoring work and fully help her mentee realize she was not a poor teacher. Now, the duo is continuing to positively impact students together.

(Continued)

(Continued)

MENTOR TIP

Use Kala's story as a reminder to help understand your mentee's needs and be there as a resource for your mentee to confide in you when needed.

RECAP AND REFLECT

As mentors, it is our job to set the foundation for a strong mentor and mentee partnership. It begins with being the point person for your mentee and recalling the experiences of being a new teacher yourself. As you consider shifting to a student-centered planning routine, also consider the directional supports that can guide the differentiation needs of your mentees. Figure 2.7 summarizes possibilities for each area based on this chapter's information. Use those ideas and add onto the possibilities as you reflect further on your mentor learning. Last but not least, tap into the use of strengths-based feedback in order to propel the partnership further. Together, this will empower beginning teachers to take actionable steps that motivate their students to learn and grow.

Figure 2.7 Summary Table of Directional Support Ideas

Emotional	Communication	Physical	Instructional
• Self-care routines • Student trauma • Social-emotional needs pertinent to age levels • Start a journal of moments • Family stressors and challenges	• Student recognition • Student behavior • Collaborating with colleagues • Family Involvement • Parent-teacher conferences • Administrator evaluations	• Copier • Building drills • Room location • Staff meetings	• Methods • Engagement of students • Strategies and skills for students

MENTOR INQUIRY REFLECTION

Think back to the guiding questions at the beginning of the chapter. Take some time to reflect on the questions that follow as well as use the Rubric for Student-Centered Mentoring, Section #2 to help set goals and make a plan (Figure 2.8).

1. What areas do you want to consider as you begin the work of mentoring?

2. How can you promote positive thoughts with students, colleagues, and yourself?

3. How can you be supportive and give feedback at the same time?

4. Which Student-Centered Mentoring success criteria would you choose to support your mentoring partnership?

5. What are some initial action steps you can take to achieve a more positive and supportive relationship?

Figure 2.8 Rubric for Student-Centered Mentoring

#2: Build Positive and Supportive Relationships With Mentees		
Beginner	**Emerging**	**Innovative**
The mentor is interested in helping beginning teachers and either has not fully developed facilitation skills for any type of support and/or is in the beginning stages of forming a relationship.	The mentor is working toward being a positive resource who is attempting to use supportive conversational skills and expanding the use of feedback strategies.	The mentor is a partner with the beginning teacher, consistently showing effective communication skills that result in a successful working relationship.

Success Criteria

- I can be a point person for my mentee and provide my mentee direction whenever needed.
- I can identify the type of support my mentee may need depending on the moment.
- I can support positive communication with colleagues by being a model for my mentee.
- I can be a listener and seek to ask questions rather than always jumping to reply in conversations.
- I can use feedback that is building on the strengths of my mentee.

3

BUILDING EFFICACY WITH NEW TEACHERS AND MENTORS

Teaching is something many tend to think we do in isolation. When I was a new teacher, my heart would drop every time an adult would open my classroom door. What were they thinking about my teaching, my classroom, my students? How many of you still feel this way? I thought I needed to plan and execute everything perfectly to demonstrate that students were learning. I did not realize the true power in collective efficacy until I connected it to a sport I was learning: powerlifting. Through the experience of learning to powerlift, I developed a belief in myself, especially when others were watching. Powerlifting is a type of weightlifting focused on building strength in three types of lifts, and even though one person is lifting at a time, help from others is required to complete each lift. Many may not see powerlifting as a group sport, but I definitely needed encouragement and instruction from others to learn how to squat, bench, and deadlift without hurting myself. When I began this type of lifting, I was very guarded in what I was willing to try in front of others. Slowly, my confidence grew and my mindset changed. Surprisingly, I continue to want to learn more and am able to attempt certain lifts and higher weights without worrying as much about others watching. I realized that the same was true for my teaching career. This openness carried over to my teaching. I found I needed to tap into the power of my community of support to improve what I was doing in my own practice—no matter what new skill or role I learn. The teaching profession is becoming more and more of a collaborative job. This requires vulnerability to believe in our efforts along with the help of others.

In this chapter, we will explore the second layer of Student-Centered Mentoring: collective mindset (Figure 3.1). We will reflect on our beliefs about joint partnerships with our mentees and how we can build collective efficacy together. Self-efficacy and collective efficacy are interdependent of each other. Collective efficacy improves instructional practice, which boosts feelings of self-efficacy. Teachers' beliefs about themselves and their practices have an enormous impact on student learning. It is vital to promote a collective mindset through the mentoring partnership in order to increase our mentee's confidence and their effectiveness of instructional practices.

Figure 3.1 Layers of Student-Centered Mentoring With Key Ideas

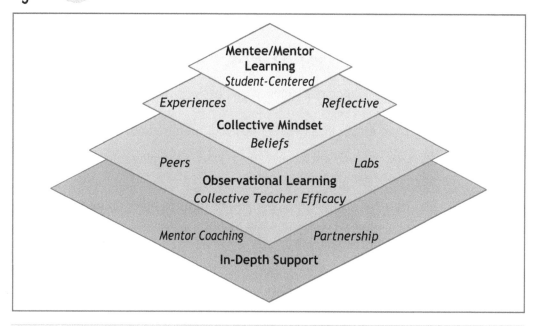

WHAT IS THIS CHAPTER ABOUT?

In this chapter, you will learn strategies to

➤ Reflect together on beliefs

➤ Build an innovative learning mindset

➤ Promote a classroom of independent learners

The purpose of this chapter is to give you strategies to help promote collective teacher efficacy with your mentees. This starts with the beliefs and mindset work of new teachers that they can use with their students, like establishing a learning mindset or promoting independent thinking. Three main categories come to the surface that supports efficacious new teachers: a learning mindset, brain-based learning, and reflecting on our impact. As teachers, having an innovative learning mindset can be modeled for students and enhances student motivation. This work can then connect with responding to students of all cultures by supporting brain-based learning, making it equitable to beginning teachers in rural areas as well as suburbs and cities. Let's uncover a few tips that can support this endeavor for not only us but also students and our colleagues.

MENTOR INQUIRY PRE-REFLECTION

Use these guiding questions as you explore the ideas in this chapter:

1. What efficacious beliefs does your mentee hold about themself?

2. How can you encourage an innovative learning mindset with your mentee and their students?

3. How can you encourage mentees to learn more about fostering independent learners while increasing their culturally responsive skillset?

THE IMPORTANCE OF TEACHER BELIEFS AND SELF-EFFICACY

Teacher beliefs are dependent on successful moments, and beliefs can even more so stem from emotional experiences. Positive and negative beliefs then form a teacher's view of the impact that can be made on students. This is why it is important to assist beginning teachers in building their confidence and self-efficacy at the start of their career. "When teachers have greater self-efficacy, they work harder to design mastery experiences and that in turn increases students' self-efficacy" (Donohoo, 2017, p. 15). Stronger instructional practices, effective classroom management, and promoting positive social-emotional experiences and motivation to learn will then blend together to result in a thriving classroom.

Where can beliefs start to go off track the most? Stress from emotional moments. Emotional experiences, or teacher trauma, usually stems from our worry about students. While still in the classroom, most nights I would lay awake hoping and praying for all of my kids. I still have dreams. I still tear up thinking about my students. I still wish for them to be healthy and safe. Those worries were not ever going to go away because those worries are a by-product of developing relationships with students. If we let it, the risk of empathy can take a toll on efficacy and teaching practices.

Some teachers experience more traumatic moments than others, which affects if we believe we can teach all students or not. "For teachers, who are directly exposed to a large number of young people with trauma in their work, a secondary type of trauma, known as vicarious trauma, is a big risk" (Minero, 2017). As mentors, it is our job to help beginning teachers recognize the signs of this kind of trauma. Vicarious trauma affects teachers' brains the same as their students' by emitting a response of fear—excessive cortisol and adrenaline resulting in an increase in heart rate, blood pressure, respiration, and a flood of emotions (Minero, 2017). The result is often that teachers question their ability to impact students' learning or even end up leaving the profession entirely.

Stressful moments are compounded for new teachers, as their confidence is lower and experiences are limited. How can a new teacher learn to devise a high sense of efficacy—confidence in their ability to affect student learning despite all outside factors? A mentor can help by not only supporting emotional needs but also by encouraging a collective mindset. Mindset beliefs can be fully developed through visualizing and by doing what is in our realm of control, which in turn we want to also promote for students. The focus on what is in our control will affect what impact can be made on our students' learning while meeting students' emotional and social needs as well. As a teacher, we are unable to control that a student may not have heat or supervision. What do we have control of within the four walls of the classroom?

MENTOR TIP

Watch out for potential moments that could cause trauma with your mentee. A few possible topics could center around a homeless student, evaluation from an administrator, and so forth.

SETTING THE STAGE FOR COLLECTIVE TEACHER EFFICACY IN YOUR MENTORING PARTNERSHIP

The foundation has to be set for how to develop individual efficacious beliefs in order to understand collective teacher efficacy. Both concepts are supportive of each other and can be built simultaneously. The strategies in this chapter support beginning teachers' efficacious beliefs and actions. By working through them together as mentor and mentee, the joint efforts foster a stronger sense of collective teacher efficacy in your mentor partnership. Why is this so important? If we want to help beginning teachers succeed, then encouraging collective efficacy is key in impacting their confidence. Secondly, collective teacher efficacy not only ranks the highest in John Hattie's Visible Learning research, currently at an effect size of 1.39, but it's also what matters most in raising student achievement (Donohoo, 2017; Hattie, 2020).

An effective mentoring partnership is a perfect example of collective efficacy. Jenni Donohoo's work outlines further the conditions of collective efficacy with staff, and she shares the importance of the four sources of efficacy in this order: mastery experiences, vicarious experiences, social persuasion, and affective states (Bandura, 1986; Donohoo, 2017; Goddard et al., 2004). Figure 3.2

Figure 3.2 The Connection Between Student-Centered Mentoring Layers and Collective Teacher Efficacy Sources

	Collective Efficacy Definition	Layers of Support	Mentoring Connections
Mastery Experiences	Trying something as a team and seeing success because of their actions	• Collective mindset • Partner cycles	Learning and growing together, achieving success resulting in increased confidence as a team; meets needs for instructional support
Vicarious Experiences	Seeing others trying something and seeing success; making the connection they too can overcome challenges	• New teacher and mentor learning • Collective mindset • Labs and observations • Partner cycles	Planning lessons and observing colleagues, group inquiry and collaboration, case study of students, connected to all support types
Social Persuasion	Credible and trustworthy colleague persuades a team to try something new and overcome obstacles	• New teacher and mentor learning • Collective mindset • Partner cycles	Student-centered training, learning with colleagues in similar roles, triad collaboration with coach, increase in communication support along with emotional area
Affective States	Feeling successful when overcoming difficulty or anxiety about potential	• Collective mindset • Partner cycles	Collaborative reflection, problem-solving next steps, celebration of student growth; a result of emotional support

Adapted from Donohoo (2017)

connects the layers of Student-Centered Mentoring to the states of collective teacher efficacy. From my experience, the sources of collective teacher efficacy are all equally important when we consider the directional support required to guide new teachers in their beginning years. The layer of collective mindset can be seen in all source areas.

> ## 💡 MENTOR TIP
>
> Take note of ways to incorporate a variety of collective teacher efficacy sources in the experiences for your mentee, starting with affective states. Think back to Chapter 2 about the importance of having emotional support in place of north on a compass, which will result in you and your mentee achieving affective states.

THE STRATEGIES FOR DEVELOPING EFFICACY

This chapter's strategies give some efficacy building ideas so that you can have collective teacher efficacy present in your mentoring partnership. As a mentor, you are vital in encouraging your mentee's positive beliefs and an innovator learning mindset. A teacher's belief in their potential pairs with how they approach learning. New teacher's beliefs and impact are connected to the effective support from mentors (Brueggeman, 2018). Teachers will be able to positively impact student achievement if they believe they are capable of having the ability to impact all of their students. That can be your result by employing all of the strategies. Specifically, Strategies 2, 3, and 5 contain multiple action steps that will give you more ways to continue mixing in different collective teacher efficacy sources. In the end, you will be empowered to make more of an impact on mentee's as well as students' growth and learning.

STRATEGY #1: REFLECT TOGETHER ON BELIEFS

Mentor teachers who have developed a high sense of self-efficacy have the confidence in their students to overcome their struggles and to increase achievement. This mindset can then be passed along to mentees, which results in collective teacher efficacy. Collective teacher efficacy is the level to which teachers believe in their group's efforts to contribute to students' achievement and provide their group with instructional best practices they can utilize throughout their careers (Bandura, 1997; Goddard et al., 2000; McCoach & Colbert, 2014). Helping mentees develop efficacious beliefs includes reflection on statements that relate to their views about how they impact their students (Figure 3.3).

Figure 3.3 Efficacy Beliefs Self-Reflection

Belief Statements	Self-Assessment Rating		
I believe all students have the ability to learn.	Never	Sometimes	Always
I am confident I can motivate all students to learn.	Never	Sometimes	Always
I am well prepared to teach the information I am assigned to teach.	Never	Sometimes	Always
Learning takes place in my classroom because students are not worried about external factors in their home life.	Never	Sometimes	Always
If a student in my classroom does not learn something the first time, we will try to find another way.	Never	Sometimes	Always
It takes a collaborative effort to positively impact student learning.	Never	Sometimes	Always
I am willing to try new methods to better meet the needs of my students.	Never	Sometimes	Always
It is important to have conversations with colleagues about student learning.	Never	Sometimes	Always
I like to observe other classrooms in order to grow my repertoire of instructional strategies.	Never	Sometimes	Always

Belief Statements	Self-Assessment Rating		
I will ask for feedback from another colleague, instructional coach, principal, or students.	Never	Sometimes	Always
I have developed ways to cope when a stressful situation arises with students.	Never	Sometimes	Always
I balance my time working with students and self-care throughout my day.	Never	Sometimes	Always

Using this self-reflection can help mentees gain confidence in their ability to handle information about students, especially their home lives. This reflection also helps them understand the power of our thinking and how we can make an impact on all students in our classrooms.

I recommend having your mentee complete the belief rating a few times a year as well as you self-reflecting to then compare your thinking together. Base periodic conversations with your mentee around their efficacious beliefs in-between self-reflections. The reflections and conversations are what fosters the growth of collective teacher efficacy, which we will go deeper into throughout the chapter.

 MENTOR TIP

Find opportunities to revisit the efficacy beliefs periodically throughout the school year. Also, before the year is over, reflect again and compare your results to the beginning of the year self-reflection.

STRATEGY #2: REFLECT ON INSTRUCTIONAL IMPACT WITH YOUR MENTEE

"Kids need us to believe in them and then hold them accountable." Andi Swatner, an elementary reading interventionist and colleague, shared this thought with me as we had a conversation about being responsive to students and then seeing an impact on their learning. For any teacher, visualizing our instructional impact is not always an easy task. The desire to know our impact is what starts the process. John Hattie and his colleagues have done a great deal of research around the statement of "Knowing thy impact." There are many ways to get involved with the Visible Learning work, but as a beginning teacher, it can all seem very overwhelming to investigate as well as to put into action. A mentor can help guide where to start and how to implement that kind of endeavor.

KEEPING IT STUDENT CENTERED

You may already be tempted to second-guess your own instructional practices as a teacher; instead try taking the lens of your students to continue to grow in your craft. This approach can be modeled for your mentee, as you respond to students based on your impact in the classroom.

ACTION STEP #1: HELP YOUR MENTEE BUILD A ROUTINE OF EVALUATING IMPACT

As teachers, if we want to impact our students, we have to learn more about effective instructional practices and continually ask ourselves, "What is my impact?" This question has been my starting point with many teachers. I had to have the help of others to get where I am today and asked many questions to receive appropriate guidance on how to best help all students. Asking questions to learn more from teammates is a key part of effective planning and problem solving. For some, asking questions can evoke uncertainty and vulnerability. Having the courage to say, "We don't know," is hard. It shows we are not perfect. As learners, if we want to grow and understand, we have to ask questions about new skills and our impact. This mindset is the first of the 10 Mindframes for Visible Learning: "I am an evaluator of my impact on student learning" (Hattie, 2018).

You will want to include reflection about impact and model thinking aloud in your mentoring conversations. In order to develop this routine for evaluating impact, first look at the Teaching Impact Self-Reflection (Figure 3.4). The belief statements are similar to another mindframe, "I am a change agent and believe all students can improve" (Hattie & Zierer, 2018). This particular mindframe correlates with details from the Student-Centered Mentoring Learning Mindset Progressions from Chapter 2 and with culturally responsive teaching practices. You can pick one or all of the belief statements to help support deeper discussions about impact. Correlations that some mentors and mentees have made with this reflection are increased student motivation and more effective management in a student-centered classroom.

Figure 3.4 Teaching Impact Self-Reflection

Belief Statements	Self-Assessment Rating		
I am able to apply successful methods to differentiate my teaching.	Never	Sometimes	Always
I am successful with using a variety of strategies to increase my students' motivation.	Never	Sometimes	Always
I believe that my teaching can have an impact on students.	Never	Sometimes	Always
I know to research and ask about various strategies to enhance students' motivation.	Never	Sometimes	Always
I strive to have an impact on students through my teaching.	Never	Sometimes	Always
I strive to always encourage students in their learning.	Never	Sometimes	Always
I am confident that my teaching has a positive impact on students.	Never	Sometimes	Always
I understand I need to regularly reflect on the impact of my teaching.	Never	Sometimes	Always

Adapted from Hattie and Zierer (2018)

MENTOR TIP

The 10 Mindframes for Visible Learning are a great place to explore to learn more about evaluating impact. I suggest looking into them later on in the mentoring partnership and add on a few mindframes at a time.

The mindframe work strongly connects to efficacy and responding to various students' cultures. Hattie (Hattie & Zierer, 2018) explores the abbreviation of DIE (diagnosis, intervention, evaluation) within the mindframe of evaluating impact on student learning. Diagnosis, intervention, and evaluation can maximize a teacher's impact on their students. The first step of evaluating impact consists of a teacher diagnosing what each student brings to the lesson, his or her motivations, and willingness to engage. It relates strongly to our mindset and culture work! Next, if one intervention for a student does not work then change to another. I associate taking the time to truly see change as well as encouraging students to be independent in the process with the intervention phase. Lastly, you would evaluate through multiple methods and collaborate with your mentee around the amount of impact from the interventions. This final phase would be further supportive of brain-based learning as well as fostering collective efficacy.

KEEPING IT STUDENT CENTERED

Diagnose, intervene, and evaluate—consider this process as you plan with your mentee about what independent and innovative learning to achieve student growth looks like in their classroom.

ACTION STEP #2: BUILD SELF-EFFICACY TOGETHER THROUGH RECOGNITION OF EFFECTIVE INSTRUCTIONAL STRATEGIES

A valuable start for beginning teachers to practice effective instruction is to recognize how to best influence students. How do you guide mentees in confidently and effectively choosing strong practices? Teach them how to utilize the Visible Learning Strategies in support of their beliefs. The research of the Visible Learning Strategies has been shown to showcase a wealth of instructional strategies and their effects on increased student-learning outcomes.

MENTOR TIP

Go to the Visible Learning MetaX website and explore the information about the instructional strategies research on a compilation of effect sizes.

Understanding that effect sizes are based on the 0.4 hinge point first requires a quick tutorial. Explain the growth students can make that is equivalent to a year's worth of time in relation to 0.4. Any strategy above that 0.4 hinge point could have the potential of being more than a year's worth of growth for a student. The strategy influences are based on the finding from thousands of meta-analyses and studies. With the 250 or more strategies in the mix, how do you know which one to focus on first? Here is a possible protocol for using the strategies list with your mentee:

Steps for Analyzing Visible Learning Strategies

1. Think of student makeup

2. Narrow to student and student-learning list

3. Pick a few to dive into based on effect size

KEEPING IT STUDENT CENTERED

Try the protocol out with your own group of students prior to using it with your mentee. Make the connection to mindsets and think about using the information in conjunction with the DIE (diagnose, intervene, evaluate) process.

STRATEGY #3: ESTABLISH AN INNOVATIVE LEARNING MINDSET TO GROW OUR IMPACT

Since our beliefs about impacting student achievement are important, then our mindset about learning is an integral factor in affecting students' learning. This is a valuable step for you to take as a mentor and to help your mentee as well. The work of Carol Dweck and George Couros is very interesting in relation to mindset. Belief that abilities, intelligence, and talents are developed leading to the creation of new and better ideas is Carol Dweck's growth mindset approach:

> Mindset change is not about picking up a few pointers here and there. It's about seeing things in a new way. When people change to a growth mindset, they change from a judge-and-be-judged framework to a learn-and-help-learn framework. Their commitment is to growth, and growth takes plenty of time, effort, and mutual support.

> —Carol S. Dweck, *Mindset: The New Psychology of Success*

The three components for growth—time, effort, and support—encourage true learning. With those three pieces, anyone can learn. Now let's add on the notion of innovation. I find George Couros' (2015) characteristics of an innovator's mindset—empathetic, problem finders, risk-takers, networked, observant, creators, resilient, and reflective—embody the essential components to create meaningful learning experiences for all of those around us. Having the courage to say, "We don't know," comes to mind and is desired with an innovative mindset. All teachers, mentors, and beginning teachers need to have courage to reflect on their own learning mindset to believe in making a difference for their students.

With a learning mindset, innovative learners employ certain characteristics. To start with, the learner being empowered to attempt new problems needs to be coupled with being passionate about improving critical thinking skills. All of this has to happen while being flexible with next steps. The possibility of failure or imperfection is a part of the process as well. A logical progression to get to the highest level of learning mindset can be seen in this way: fixed, emerging, growth, and innovator. Utilizing the combined thinking of Couros and Dweck, I have added on overall definitions and characteristics of each learning mindset component (Figure 3.5). Also included in the chart are outcomes that an individual may showcase as a part of each mindset.

Figure 3.5 Learning Mindset Definition and Characteristics

	Definition	Characteristics	Outcomes
Fixed mindset	Abilities, intelligence, and talent are constant.	• Avoid challenges • Gives up easily • Effortless • Ignores feedback • Feels threatened by others success • Seeks completion	An individual will maintain their mindset, which will most likely be lower than their full potential.
Emerging mindset	Abilities, intelligence, and talent are unbalanced.	• Uncertain about risks • Anxious • Inconsistent effort • Varies with feedback • Follower • Seeks acceptance	An individual may make slight increases in attainment of knowledge or skill.

	Definition	Characteristics	Outcomes
Growth mindset	Abilities, intelligence, and talent can be developed.	• Embraces challenge • Persistent • Effort equals mastery • Learns from feedback • Inspired by others' success • Seeks perfection	An individual can get smarter or reach high levels of achievement.
Innovator mindset	Abilities, intelligence, and talents can be developed, leading to the creation of new and better ideas.	• Empathetic • Problem-solution finders • Resilient risk-takers • Reflective collaborators • Flexible experimentation • Passionate • Seeks improvement	An individual can be empowered to seek creativity and be critical thinkers, at times with a team approach.

Adapted from Dweck (2016) and Couros (2015).

MENTOR TIP

As you explore learning mindsets with your mentee, also promote them to step out of their comfort zone. Encourage them to take on a collaborative, or team stance, toward learning. This is important to also model for students, as, "Two heads are better than one!"

Can you be in a different mindset based on your different experiences? Yes. Can you move in and out of a mindset throughout your learning? Yes again. Moving from fixed to growth and innovative is more about the process than always being an innovator. More so than anything, it is about stepping outside of your comfort zone—be comfortable with being uncomfortable in your learning. Among other benefits, Nowik (2015) shares that you will make growth, have a desire to challenge yourself more, and increase your self-confidence when you take the steps outside of your comfort zone. This benefits both you and your mentee, as it all supports a positive belief system. The learning mind-set work molds a beginning teacher's beliefs so that they can also implement professional learning and in turn continue to increase their efficacy. The job of a mentor is to help with the investigation of a learning mindset and guide mentees through their exploration. This work will then lead to building student collective efficacy as well.

ACTION STEP #1: SET GOALS WITH A LEARNING MINDSET PROGRESSION

Many of my colleagues know I like setting goals. I also absolutely love making lists. (Who doesn't feel good when they accomplish their to-do list?!) I set goals in conjunction with my lists, big and small, to have a clear direction and to keep me on track. When working with teachers, I encourage them to set goals in their work that focus on their impact on students. This helps keep the attention on not only the students' needs and their learning but also on the teacher's desired skills. Goal setting is one of the main ways to support your mentee's growth and propel their learning forward faster. Goal setting is also one of the key ways to support the effectiveness of a mentoring partnership. Review the Learning Mindset Progression with Success Criteria table in Figure 3.6. Begin by reflecting on the category you mostly fall in and then select one or two of the criteria to help you move into another category closer to the innovator side. Then, assist your mentee in using a similar process.

Figure 3.6 **Learning Mindset Progression With Success Criteria**

Fixed	Emerging	Growth	Innovator
The learner is accepting of the current mindset and will maintain skills and knowledge without questions or risk-taking.	The learner is uncertain about attempting new skills and may work little by little to make small improvements.	The learner is inspired to increase achievement and is persistent in mastering new skills.	The learner is empowered to attempt to solve new problems and is passionate about improving critical thinking skills while being flexible with next steps.

Success Criteria

- I can set a focused goal and revise when needed.
- I can listen to feedback and take action in attainable steps.
- I can try out something new in manageable chunks.
- I can make time to ask questions and be creative.
- I can celebrate the easy and difficult steps in my practices.

KEEPING IT STUDENT CENTERED

Take on a student-centered inquiry with the Learning Mindset Progression to set beginning goals and support growth toward being an innovator. For example, try it when working with a small group of students by reflecting with students on their own mindsets. The students can learn this skill together and employ the aspect of a team approach. With the students being our focus, then all teachers can make a difference by employing this kind of a learning mindset.

We can't be afraid to revise our goals when needed. The whole concept of learning at an innovative mindset requires change. Change is personal. We have to put aside our assumptions and take risks to try new ideas. This mindset begs for vulnerability. That means the majority of what we do won't be perfect and will take multiple attempts. We owe it to our students to be models of this! With all of that said, it means our goals will be imperfect and will need revision at times as well.

To further help mentees see the learning mindset work as impactful, pair your goal setting with discussions. Have conversations about what learning looks like so you can provide more insight and build on beliefs. See the activity in Figure 3.7 for a possible process to use with beginning teachers to have in-depth conversations around learning mindset. This is what it could look like in practice—with an article that includes a similar message from this chapter as well as a video to spark further thinking. Another option is to also consider using parts of the activity.

Figure 3.7 Learning Inquiry Activity

1. Have teachers answer and discuss questions about learning.

   What does learning look like in your mind?

   - Is learning sometimes hard?
   - Does learning have a problem?
   - Can you fail when you learn?
   - How do you feel about learning when asked to explain your reasoning, when you have to try something again, and when you don't understand?
   - Define a learning mindset.

(Continued)

(Continued)

2. Read the article, "Mindset to Believe."

3. Watch the video from Khan Academy (2014), "You Can Learn Anything" https://www.youtube.com/watch?v=JC82Il2cjqA

4. Discuss definitions of a learning mindset.

5. Reflect on having a learning mindset using the Learning Mindset Progression

6. Share reflections of the Learning Mindset Progression.

There is no reward without risks or failure. The process of learning comes with chances, imperfection, and messiness. Many say that's where the real learning takes place. It is where we learn persistence and flexibility. It is where we learn problem solving and creativity. It is where our thought process behind our actions grows. It is where we develop beliefs. That sounds amazing and beautiful! So embrace the imperfect and celebrate the process along the way! Whether you achieve your goal or not, you can still have fun trying.

IN THE CLASSROOM

In order to include a true focus on students, promote the use of a similar learning inquiry with students. Modifications can be made to have the same conversations with even the youngest of learners. For example, a discussion in a kindergarten class was centered around these three questions posted on an anchor chart:

- Is learning hard?

- Does learning have a problem?

- Can you fail?

Don't forget to teach students to set goals as well! Goal setting is one of the most influential ways to support students' growth and propel their learning forward faster.

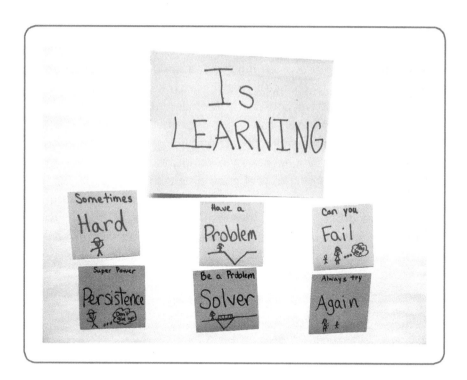

ACTION STEP #2: ENCOURAGE MENTEES TO TAKE TIME TO GROW

Time. Where does it all go? I certainly wish for more of it, that's for sure. Time is a resource that people continually say they want more of. Whether it is more time to prepare, to finish a project, or with students, the key words are *more time.* I honestly wonder if there is a black hole for it! Our minds are constantly thinking about time, and we are deeply connected to a biological clock. For any educator, the desire of more time is exponential. For beginning teachers, it is an even stronger desire. In the numerous meetings, classrooms, and learning opportunities I get to participate in, I constantly hear time is a factor. So if time is looked at as a deficit, then taking time to learn something new will be perceived as difficult to do as well. But it takes time to learn. It takes time to change.

How is time connected to learning mindsets? Take a look at the pull of the mindsets (Figure 3.8). When thinking about the time needed to accomplish a task, an obstacle, or learning something new, some approach that with the mindset, "It can be done!" Others believe it is impossible to change. It is a tug-of-war game with time in the middle. As we are more willing and hopeful while asking positive questions, time gives way to more of an innovator's mindset. We are allowing ourselves the time to change by acting with a growth mindset. The opposite happens if we constantly feel defeated by time. We are pulled into a fixed mindset as we get overwhelmed by the stress of day-to-day work and are more doubtful about getting our tasks done. This is coupled then by a negative viewpoint, and we start to ask ourselves, are we ever going to feel good about our teaching? This may lead us to wonder whether we can ever make a difference with our students. The other aspect of this issue then directs us toward the opposite of willingness. If a new teacher wants material just handed to them, do they ever learn? This line of thinking results in low receptiveness to want to learn and change.

Figure 3.8   Learning Mindset and Time Tug-of-War

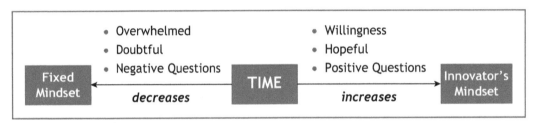

As mentors, we can encourage hopefulness with mentees. To remain hopeful means we have to try to think positively about our time. I reflect back on wanting more time with students because time is precious in the classroom. I wish to always have the mindset to think positively about believing I can make a difference. Otherwise, I just wasted my time thinking I can't, and that doesn't help anyone succeed. That carries over to then wanting to take time to learn. Being hopeful also includes celebrating along the way. Remember to celebrate the process and the little parts of learning, which we will talk more about in Chapter 4.

Understanding that change takes time requires us to balance that time in order to increase our learning mindset. We all want more time to make changes. Change requires balancing what we already know with taking on new learning. This is just like balance is recommended between working and taking care of ourselves. I am still working on that one, as I know many are! It honestly is like being lost in a forest; we have to sometimes stop to rest. This idea of finding balance has made me reflect on where balance needs to be in taking time to adjust our mindset.

Prioritizing time is a huge part of the balancing act of our day. You will want to encourage your mentee to find ways to stay on track and analyze what tasks are most important. What are our priorities as teachers, especially if we are new? There may be things we want to do in our classrooms or lessons, but we are unsure of where to begin. The question of prioritization came to me when I first recognized beginning teachers trying to "do it all." Mentors can help by encouraging mentees to prioritize a daily to-do list. Prioritization lies at the heart of feeling like we do have more time with students to make an impact on their learning. Focusing on learning and relationships are a must with students and colleagues. Learning and relationships coincide. It will greatly benefit your mentee and reiterate at least the feeling of using time wisely! Consider these questions as you talk with mentees in how to prioritize their day-to-day lessons and focus:

➤ How much time do we have for the lesson/activity?

➤ What are the high-yield/high-effect size instructional practices that will make the most of the allotted time?

➤ Will the times work for everything?

➤ What does the time look like? Sound like?

➤ Can I get everything done in that small amount of time?

➤ Do I have any time left?

MENTOR TIP

Make it a priority to check on how and what your mentee prioritizes from day-to-day. I am the queen of making lists to help me stay on track, which is why sticky notes and Google Keep are so valuable to me in visualizing my important tasks first. You can think about embedding this into a conversation at least once a month.

Revisit the time tug-of-war and replace each end with hope and stress. Which do you want to win: hope or stress? In the end, we are still hoping to balance the time that leads us to successful teaching and learning. Considering our time is such a valuable resource, we want to continue to focus on what helps us get to the true nature of our role as teachers.

IN THE CLASSROOM

We can take this balance of time process and use it in similar discussions with students. Think of using the preceding questions as well as encouraging students with the following:

● What should we prioritize? At school and at home?

● How do we encourage each other to be hopeful about learning as well as change?

In order to understand that change takes time, we have to continuously model this process for students as well.

STRATEGY #4: SET THE STAGE TO FOSTER INDEPENDENT LEARNERS

Now that we have thought about growing an innovative learning mindset, let's uncover how the actions of a teacher can accelerate a classroom of independent learners. This is extremely important, as you want to support your mentee's beliefs in their actions to promote students' learning. Shift your attention to what learning looks and sounds like—the action of learning. It is important as new teachers to identify what learning characteristics we should embody and expect from our students. Visualize the sights and sounds of a classroom.

➤ Are students expecting the teacher to give them the information they need?

➤ Are students unable to problem-solve before asking for help?

➤ Are students fearful of getting something wrong?

If you replied yes to any of those, then the students are dependent learners. Dependent learners will more than likely possess a fixed mindset, possibly even an emerging mindset at times. On the other hand, independent learners maintain either growth or innovator's mindsets, where persistence and resilience are key to how to approach learning. Hammond (2015) compares what it looks like to be dependent and independent learners in her book *Culturally Responsive Teaching and The Brain*. See Figure 3.9.

Figure 3.9 The Dependent Learner Versus Independent Learner

Dependent Learner	Independent Learner
• Is dependent on the teacher to carry most of the cognitive load of a task always	• Relies on the teacher to carry some of the cognitive load temporarily
• Is unsure of how to tackle a new task	• Utilizes strategies and processes for tackling a new task
• Cannot complete a task without scaffolds	• Regularly attempts new tasks without scaffolds
• Will sit passively and wait if stuck until teacher intervenes	• Has cognitive strategies for getting unstuck
• Doesn't retain information well or "doesn't get it"	• Has learned how to retrieve information from long-term memory

Printed with permission from Hammond (2015)

KEEPING IT STUDENT CENTERED

You may be thinking that you should give this information to your mentee using a direct approach. However, remember to take a student-centered approach through your questioning in conversations and try giving strengths-based feedback to your mentee when you hear that their students are acting as independent learners.

Teachers with a growth and innovator's mindset have the passion and perseverance to instruct students. However, they need more than grit to help students. Discussing how learning also looks is a step that will keep the passion and perseverance alive as beginning teachers continue through their career. A key component of viewing learning is encouraging mentees to be independent learners in the learning process throughout their entire career. This is something to consider when approaching the directional supports, and you may want to encourage a focus in this area. Spending time discussing learning beliefs can help guide your mentee in what to look for and can accelerate student learning in a beginning teacher's classroom. If seeing learning in action is a desire for your mentee, look ahead to Chapter 5. Just remember, this is no easy task for your mentee to identify out of the gate and ensure them that relying on colleagues will help. Here are some questions to use in conversation with your mentee about promoting independent learners:

- What does learning look like?

- What does engagement look like? Sound like?

- How can all students be independent in their learning?

- How does the classroom environment support all students? Students with trauma? Students of different cultures? Students with learning difficulties?

- In what ways do our students in front of us learn?

- How do we get to know our students through our teaching?

IN THE CLASSROOM

It is vital to partner with students in creating the condition for independence. As a mentor, help build capacity for mentees with this work to move students from being dependent to independent learners. The same questions for promoting independent learners can be used with students. You might also consider making a T-chart with students, comparing their views of a dependent and independent learner.

STRATEGY #5: PROMOTE EQUITABLE PRACTICES THAT REINFORCE A MENTEE'S SELF-EFFICACY

Helping a mentee develop the mindset that he or she can help ALL students takes time. One way to help your mentee develop this mindset and boost self-efficacy is to promote culturally responsive actions that provide access to all learners. Research in culturally responsive methods concludes that it is not just an approach or framework that teachers can use to "get students to learn" or "fix their struggles." This deficit thinking is exactly what leads teachers to question both their self-efficacy and students' efficacious beliefs in the ability to learn. As Hollie (2013) puts it, being culturally responsive is the opposite of the sink-or-swim approach to traditional schools. Both mentors and schools can support beginning teachers with adjusting to the idea of being culturally responsive in connection to providing effective and engaging instruction that leads our students toward being independent learners. This includes helping teachers become aware of their students' backgrounds, home environments, and cultural/familial values and to see those as positive contributions that they bring to the classroom and to their collective learning experiences rather than focusing on what students "don't have" or "haven't learned yet." To do this means we are continually revisiting our own belief system about all students' learning along with the instructional practices, routines, and norms that we use within our classrooms.

 KEEPING IT STUDENT CENTERED

It may be tricky to navigate difficult conversations about culture and diversity with your mentee. You have the courage in you to be vulnerable in sharing how your thinking has changed as an educator. Recall the sources of collective teacher efficacy and the connection to the layers of Student-Centered Mentoring earlier in the chapter—social persuasion and affective states!

ACTION STEP #1: SET A MEETING WITH YOUR MENTEE AND BRAINSTORM A CULTURALLY RESPONSIVE DEFINITION

How do we foster an environment for independent learners? Being culturally responsive in our teaching practices will allow students to flourish. Here's a question many ask, "What is culturally responsive instruction?" A group of beginning teachers I worked with was exploring this area and was unsure of where to start looking. They found that the term encompasses more than race or skin color. They also found that there are many variations of the term. They also found that they had a hard time narrowing in on just one definition, and so did I! Here is a list of the most notable researchers' interpretation (Figure 3.10). In order to help your mentee understand this concept, set up a meeting and read through the definitions.

Figure 3.10 Culturally Responsive Definitions

Culturally Responsive Instruction Is . . .	
Gloria Ladson-Billing	"A pedagogy that empowers students intellectually, socially, emotionally, and politically by using cultural and historical referents to convey knowledge, to impart skills, and to change attitudes." Ladson-Billings (2009)
Geneva Gay	"The use of cultural knowledge, prior experiences, frames of reference, and performance styles of ethnically diverse students to make learning encounters more relevant to, and effective for, them." Gay (2010)
Sharroky Hollie	Adds linguistically to the term = Culturally and Linguistically Responsiveness "The validation and affirmation of indigenous (home) culture and language for the purpose of building and bridging the students to success in the culture of academia and in mainstream society." Hollie (2013)
Zaretta Hammond	"An educator's ability to recognize students' cultural displays of learning and meaning making and respond positively and constructively with teaching moves that use cultural knowledge as a scaffold to connect what the student knows to new concepts and content in order to promote effective information processing. All the while, the educator understands the importance of being in a relationship and having a social-emotional connection to the student in order to create a safe space for learning." Hammond (2015)

ACTION STEP #2: MAKE A PLAN FOR FOSTERING A CULTURALLY RESPONSIVE CLASSROOM

For new teachers, we need to make it practical and easily applicable with everything they are taking on their first year. As Bridgette, a first-year teacher asked me, "Is it even possible to be culturally responsive on day one of school?" The more professional learning I have been a part of, for topics such as trauma-informed and whole-child work, the more I understand the importance and the impact of needing to be culturally responsive to students in a way that allows us to listen to what students are saying and feeling. It ties to really getting to know our students from day 1 and having an effective classroom management plan, along with using engaging learning methods. Hollie (2013) also adds that by becoming culturally responsive in classroom management, student engagement will increase and referrals, suspensions, and expulsions will decrease. It starts with sharing identities as mentees and mentors and then doing similar work with students as developmentally appropriate. Potential areas to explore could include ethnicity, gender, religion, race, socioeconomic status, and nationality.

IN THE CLASSROOM

Brainstorm with students some ways to share identities as a community builder, not only at the beginning of the school year, but periodically revisit and add to their views throughout the year. Find ways to incorporate conversations with students about ethnicity, gender, religion, race, socioeconomic status and nationality in connection to learning objectives. Take the time to always discuss the ideas before trying them with students.

As humans, we tend to make assumptions. As teachers, we sometimes assume reasons for student behavior or noncompliance in the classroom is based on their experiences or home life. This brings about some of the efficacy belief statements: "I believe all students can learn," and "Learning takes place in my classroom because students are not worried about external factors of their home life." Whether we are confident of our impact based on having a strong agreement with those beliefs, we still have to get to know each group of students as they change from year to year.

MENTOR TIP

Consider how to guide your mentee in brainstorming ideas to inform their classroom practices as being more culturally responsive. Connect the proactive work to promoting more engaged students.

Review this question: What do we perceive a student is coming from when they arrive to school each day? I was having a conversation with my school's support interventionist, and she brought up the experience of a student being unable to describe why he was angry. After a long morning of no learning, it was discovered this student had been yelled at all morning long before arriving to school. She shared that many classroom teachers may not always be prepared to think through how to deal with this scenario. As many induction programs include building relationships as a top focus area, which is part of engaging students, it is important to know where to start when approaching a student who is dysregulated—having the inability to manage emotions. It is not easy to know how to respond to all students. Your mentor role includes being proactive in discussing ways to handle situations such as this or at least reaching out to the counselor for support.

ACTION STEP #3: HAVE CONVERSATIONS ABOUT HOW TO DEEPEN THE CULTURAL CONNECTION OF THE BRAIN AND LEARNING

Another layer of being culturally responsive includes the connection to the brain. The brain-based learning approach by Zaretta Hammond links the achievement gap to our brain and nervous system. I wish I would have known as a new teacher that the brain functions in directing learning, problem solving, and self-regulation. In order for learning to take place, a student's brain has to tell them they are safe and their teacher believes in them. "It becomes imperative to understand how to build positive social relationships that signal to the brain a sense of physical, psychological, and social safety so that learning is possible" (Hammond, 2015). Teachers need to know more than just theories at the start; teachers need to know how to combine a culture of belonging and learning with our brains all being different.

Rather than go into the technical working of the brain—dendrites, limbic region, neuroplasticity, and so on—I'll leave you with key points related to Hammond's Ready for Rigor framework in relation to the brain and moving students toward independence. In Figure 3.11, the areas from the framework have a few possible questions to pose with mentees that reinforce brain-based learning. We discussed awareness of culture earlier, but also be aware of your brain's triggers around race, gender, and culture. Helping a new teacher identify any triggers that may result in difficulty with classroom management and student engagement or areas within the emotional support will be supportive of their effectiveness.

MENTOR TIP

Take a look at the four layers with mentees and walk through the questions in the list from Figure 3.11. This will help deepen the cultural connection of the brain and learning.

Another area of importance is the cognitive mindset work with students. You can add to the processing of information by teaching cognitive routines that will signal learning shifts in the day. Connecting content to students' community and everyday lives is a simple way to support brain processing as well as to build a safe culture of learning. Build in classroom rituals around how to share learning as well, which highlights the dialogue that is inclusive of a student-centered classroom. This also supports the learning partnerships where you are giving students the language to talk about learning moves. If this work interests you further, I invite you to look into Hammond's (2015) book, *Culturally Responsive Teaching and the Brain.*

Figure 3.11   **Mentor Question Suggestions in Connection to the Ready for Rigor Framework**

Culturally Moving Brains Toward Independence	
Awareness	• What are your brain's triggers around race and culture? • What are some potential triggers that may be impeding your management of the classroom? • How do I collect student evidence that ensures all students' participation?
Information Processing	• What are some cognitive routines that will signal learning shifts in the day? • What are ideas for how I can connect content to students' community and everyday lives? • How do I intentionally plan for equitable practices that reinforce the learning of all students?
Learning Partnerships	• What are some ways we can discuss our learning, beliefs, and experiences? • What can we do to balance our time? • How can we boost students' confidence and skills of working together?
Community of Learners and Learning Environment	• What are ideas for how I can connect content to students' community and everyday lives? • What are some classroom rituals, specifically around how to share ideas? • How can we be sure all students' voices are heard in our classroom?

Adapted from Hammond (2015)

Another approach to conversations about culture and learning is helping mentees elicit feedback from students. Have mentees take the opportunity to talk with students about their perception of school, learning, and so forth. I mentioned listening to students more intuitively in Chapter 2, but we can add to that in more depth. Joy Casey, an instructional coach in Colorado, partnered with her principal to share the ways their building leveraged student voice to monitor their impact at the Annual Visible Learning Conference (Casey & Costas-Bissell, 2021). First, they helped teachers implement student surveys that included statements like, "My teacher believes in me," and "My teacher checks to make sure I understand." After the staff analyzed the results, they concentrated on a few areas in relation to their school focus and goals. "This student feedback created and fostered a positive climate and culture where every student belongs" Casey said in relation to the survey (Casey & Costas-Bissell, 2021). They also incorporated student panel interviews to add another layer to listening to students, asking questions such as, "What does it mean to have a teacher who believes in you?" and "What are some ways teachers show they believe in you?" Hearing it from kids builds the efficacious beliefs of both students and teachers.

IN THE CLASSROOM

Invite students to share thoughts in relation to their learning needs and hopes through student perception surveys, suggestion boxes, class meetings, or even schedule lunchtime chats. These options are a perfect way to promote the dialogue that embraces a student-centered environment.

FROM THE LENS OF A NEW TEACHER

How Bridgette Learned About the Power of Collective Efficacy

It was Bridgette's first year of teaching, yet she was taking a leap into a second career. Her openness and work ethic, coupled with a supportive team, had helped her to grow as an educator quickly. Erica was her mentor and was quick to say how natural Bridgette was in teaching second graders. Here is how Bridgette described her experience and related the work around her beliefs to her students as well:

As my mentor and I worked through some reading and work around developing a learning mindset, we talked about our perspective of perfection. I know I am not a perfectionist and that I am the opposite of my mentor, but that is ok. I do get nervous though when I have to explain my reasoning, whether it is right or wrong. Now I see how students feel when asked to explain their thinking and they clam up or give that frightened look. They get nervous like I do! I see that a lot in math. So I find that helping them understand how to describe the why for solving a problem a certain way can make it better.

Students don't always understand how to do a task or learn something new. This thinking really helped me to see their viewpoint because I see my students get frustrated all the time. They don't necessarily want to do it again. Building their confidence to try something again and again is important. I may not get as frustrated as easily as they do, with my mind being a little more mature than them. But that conversation with my mentor really helped me to relate to them and their viewpoint. I find myself using language stems to prompt and that does make them more willing to do things again.

Working through day-to-day teaching and with students is easier because I have Erica and my team guiding me. I appreciate the flexibility in her style to let me learn from everyone. I borrowed one teacher's math rotations idea and tried it out. I took a behavior idea from Erica in how she really talks through problems with a student. I piece things together to see what can work for me, tweaking along the way to fit my style of teaching and my classroom of students. Then if it doesn't work, I go ask for help.

Seeing herself as a learner came easy to Bridgette, and she showcased the innovator mindset needed to help her grow into an effective educator. The collaborative conversations with her mentor, Erica, and her team were also supportive in building her confidence to not give up in this profession. That is such a great example of collective efficacy!

MENTOR TIP

Share this Lens of a Mentee experience with your mentee and highlight Bridgette's perspective: See learning through students' eyes and piece together ideas to fit the students in front of you.

FROM THE LENS OF A MENTOR

How Erica Was Empowered to Learn More From Mentees

The evidence of collective efficacy noted in Bridgette's story would not be complete if we did not get to hear from her mentor, Erica, as well. This mentoring experience was Erica's third in her 27 years as an elementary teacher. She has been a mentor and a buddy to reentry teachers, and she enjoyed the role every time. Having taught for so long, she finds the value in mentoring for herself as well as new teachers. Erica's reflection of being Bridgette's mentor is empowering:

> Being a mentor is a role everyone should take on at least once in their career. Each of the mentees I have worked with has been different. I feel like I have not done as much with Bridgette, because she is such a natural. More than anything though, I don't have the mindset that mentees have to do exactly as I do. I know it would not help to tell them there is only one way to teach, or deal with a situation. I do think it is important for us to help our mentee think through all parts of a lesson, activity or situation. I know I cannot be a mentor that controls the exact next step.

> I think the area we have focused most on is how to work with students. Showing students both what they can and cannot do is my main approach. I like to walk them through what they are getting right and if they need to fix the last part to continue on learning. Students do not feel so defeated if we give specific feedback in those ways. When you teach longer, you start to notice when students need more support in these areas. It takes time. Giving Bridgette an idea or two for how to give feedback to students seems to be what she needs most. I like sharing options and giving choices for her to decide what approach to take with her students.

> I have needed Bridgette this year. Having her as my mentee came at an absolutely perfect time, because of the pandemic teaching. I get an uneasy feeling when I do not understand something, but we were able to support each other in so many ways. Bridgette helped me with using technology and allowed me to ask questions as needed. It is a good thing too, because I ask a lot of questions! I may have a lot of years in teaching, but I can always learn. And, I love learning from new teachers, like Bridgette.

Erica's willingness to be comfortable with being uncomfortable in her learning is an example of how mentors can model the same for their mentees. Even though she recognized the natural talent Bridgette has for teaching, she promoted a positive and innovator's mindset. Their conversations help build capacity for Bridgette to move students from being dependent to independent learners as well. They were excited to continue learning at this point of the process and add to their understanding of instruction through observations of other colleagues. Erica truly embodies the role of mentoring, even in year 27!

 MENTOR TIP

Use Erica's example as a model for molding your mindset, spending the time to learn how to guide students in taking learning risks.

RECAP AND REFLECT

What does it take to build our confidence in our ability to teach students? Believing we can! This chapter is helpful in providing the emotional support for beginning teachers. Beliefs are not only important to remain student centered but also in developing the skills of effective teaching. Your role as a mentor is key in guiding this work and making a lasting impact on your mentee and their students. Then, don't forget the other growth components that include effort and time. Employing an innovator's mindset will help you both grow in your teaching practices. The time spent in developing beliefs and learning mindsets will also promote effectiveness as you dive further into the layers of Student-Centered Mentoring. I encourage taking some time reading the next chapter about collaborative reflection to strengthen collective teacher efficacy within your mentoring partnership and to assist in preparation for strategies to enrich instructional support for your mentee.

MENTOR INQUIRY REFLECTION

Think back to your guiding questions at the beginning of the chapter. Take some time to reflect on the questions that follow as well as use the Rubric for Student-Centered Mentoring, Section #3, to help you set goals and make a plan for yourself (Figure 3.12).

1. What efficacious beliefs does your mentee hold about themself?

2. How can you encourage an innovative learning mindset with your mentee and their students?

3. How can you encourage mentees to learn more about fostering independent learners while increasing their culturally responsive skillset?

4. Which Student-Centered Mentoring success criteria would you choose to support your mentoring partnership?

5. What are some initial action steps you can take to achieve a more positive and supportive relationship?

Figure 3.12 Rubric for Student-Centered Mentoring

#3: Promote Collective Teacher Efficacy in a Mentoring Partnership		
Beginner	Emerging	Innovative
The mentor is working toward the belief that together an impact can be made on students but may be hesitant to fully support a group perspective.	The mentor sometimes knows students can learn as a result of the partnership and attempts to be inspired by the success of others.	The mentor believes the mentoring partnership impacts student learning because of the group's efforts to focus on students, utilizing the additional support of other colleagues.

Success Criteria

- I can seek improvement in my instructional practices.
- I can be empowered to seek creativity and take risks in front of others.
- I can support problem solving through my thinking aloud.
- I can inquire about instructional strategies that may be more effective with certain students.
- I can impact student learning despite outside factors through the help of my mentee and other colleagues.
- I can reflect on my mindset approach and increase my belief of an innovator's mindset.

4

STRENGTHENING MENTOR PARTNERSHIPS WITH COLLABORATIVE REFLECTION

The Strategies for Empowering Mentees Through Collaborative Conversations

Strategy #1: Celebrate and Reflect Together

    Action Step #1: Celebrate Growth and Success

    Action Step #2: Reflect on Practices and Revise Goals

Strategy #2: Revisit Beliefs and Equitable Expectations of Students

Strategy #3: Prepare New Teachers by Sharing Additional Experiences

    Action Step #1: Build on Experiences to Grow Your Mentee's Repertoire

    Action Step #2: Discuss Real-World Scenarios

Strategy #4: Help New Teachers Make Adjustments to Classroom Management and Student Engagement

Strategy #5: Incorporate More Discussion About Your Mentee's Impact

    Action Step #1: Collaborate Using Student Evidence

    Action Step #2: Set Up a Collaborative Inquiry With Your Mentee

Starting over as a teacher in a new district can be overwhelming. Jill is an example of this. Jill was a reentry teacher, having been in a classroom for a few years in another state before moving to Missouri. Her passion for teaching led to working her way into a new district as an instructional assistant before joining a fifth-grade team as a teacher. Despite the stress, she grew so much from the learning and guidance of her teammates. Jill recalled, "I did not have a mentor, but my team was amazing and we worked together on almost everything." The moment that really stood out to her was when she called another teammate crying. Her teammate's reply was, "You're fine! It will all be just fine!" It was in that moment that she realized collaboration was integral not only to support instruction but also when overwhelming moments get the best of you.

Teaching is a passion-driven vocation. Over the past few years of working with mentors and new teachers, that passion has been evident through the experiences that mentors have shared with me. In story after story, mentees seem to realize a trend—lean on each other rather than give up, just like Jill. What many mentors share is that it takes grit to teach and to stay in the game of teaching. Author and researcher Andrea Duckworth (2016) shares that, "Grit has two components: passion and perseverance." She further explains that talent takes effort to improve in a skill, but it also takes effort to both improve that skill and achieve. If we want our mentees to succeed, we want them to take the drive and skill to teach and continue to put in the effort to refine practices over time. As mentors, we have to support their perseverance by sharing how we have been persistent in our own experiences, along with reflecting on how we implement teaching together. This collaborative reflection is part of the second section of the Student-Centered Mentoring layers (Figure 4.1). Collectively celebrating the grit and success of teaching not only encourages your mentee's mindset but will encourage you as well.

Figure 4.1 Layers of Student-Centered Mentoring With Key Ideas

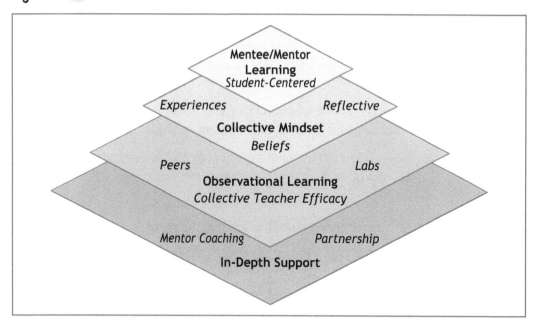

WHAT IS THIS CHAPTER ABOUT?

In this chapter, you will learn strategies to

▶ Celebrate and reflect with your mentee

▶ Share next steps based on experience

▶ Incorporate impact talk

The work of this chapter supports the key role of guiding your mentee in reflection and revision of their practices. The heart of reflection between new teachers and mentors is revisiting goals set at the beginning of the year and having conversations around student evidence. This includes revisiting belief systems and expectations for our students and us. To add onto that amazing work, we incorporate ways to share our own stories and give ideas for scenarios that promote proactive thinking about potential dilemmas your mentees could face. Walking through an inquiry cycle then adds onto the extensive thinking around solutions and opens up opportunities to add onto a student-centered learning environment. The primary focus of this chapter is to share strategies that harness the power of reflection through these opportunities with beginning teachers.

MENTOR INQUIRY PRE-REFLECTION

Use these guiding questions as you explore the ideas in this chapter:

1. How can you embed celebration and reflection of progress into your mentoring conversations?

2. What are your expectations of your mentoring partnership? What are your general expectations of students?

3. How can you share your experiences and scenarios as you have collaborative discussions with your mentee?

THE IMPORTANCE OF JOINTLY REFLECTING IN A MENTORING PARTNERSHIP

Fostering collective teacher efficacy is a continuous effort. The more collaborative your partnership becomes the higher your collective success will be for both you and your mentee. Extending your mentoring support through continuous collaboration requires a deeper focus on the sources of collective teacher efficacy in order for your mentee to feel as though they have an impact on their students.

As shared in Chapter 3, the sources of collective teacher efficacy are mastery experiences, vicarious experiences, social persuasion, and affective states. Your mentoring work includes a continuous effort to provide opportunities of the various sources when your mentee needs them. This is where the importance of collaborating comes in to play. Collaboration is evident in all sources. Collaborative reflection is also more than just having conversations together. It comes full circle with celebration and, when needed, adjustment of practices following that reflection. As a mentor, you are a model for your mentee, and that is most evident through promoting vicarious experiences and social persuasion.

Specifically related to vicarious experiences comes the explanation that if mentees see that you are successful, they too can transfer practices into daily habits successfully. This begins in your discussions where you reflect on your own experiences and expectations of students. It includes you explaining your thinking about the needs of your students and your reasoning for instructional decisions in planning.

Also consider the aspect of this source—when you have overcome challenges in your beginning years—your mentee will have an increased belief that they will be able to do the same.

Collaborative reflection is also highly supportive of social persuasion. The more cohesive your mentoring partnership, the more your mentee sees you as a credible and trustworthy colleague. As a result, they are willing to work through something new or tricky with their students and persist when either they or their students struggle.

As a result of mastery experiences, vicarious experiences, and social persuasion comes affective states. Recall that source being about feeling successful when overcoming difficulty or having anxiety about potential. If your mentee does not know if they are successful or not, then they are less confident in their abilities. You are in the perfect position to guide their identification of these feelings and helping them remain in a positive state either way.

THE STRATEGIES FOR EMPOWERING MENTEES THROUGH COLLABORATIVE CONVERSATIONS

Growth takes time and practice as well as support and collectiveness. Your mentoring role is integral in providing the opportunities for you and your mentee to have discussions about these areas throughout the mentoring experience. Through the use of the strategies in this chapter, you can enhance the mentoring relationship by providing the place, time, and modeling to have discussions that will propel students forward in your mentee's classroom. Strategies 1 and 3 dive deep into reflective conversations. The biggest difference includes revision of goals and celebration of growth in Strategy 1. This is important for the partnership and will promote a positive state of mind. You will be sharing experiences and reflecting on scenarios with the third strategy. Strategy 2 will help you both uncover your expectations of student learning, which requires further development of your beliefs. It is not just a one-time action to form beliefs but a process over time. A fourth strategy will provide guidance in next steps for your mentee to adjust management and engagement in their classroom. The final strategy of this chapter will take your collective efficacy as a partnership even further by giving you ideas in analyzing student learning together.

STRATEGY #1: CELEBRATE AND REFLECT TOGETHER

How can you encourage the recognition of the small moments throughout your mentee's journey? As a mentor, you can encourage your mentee to celebrate creative and critical thinking along the pathway of working toward goals. You can showcase the moments of vulnerability it takes to practice our craft and sing to the mountain tops when growth is made. By reflecting together, you can escalate your collective strengths and clear the path for increased impact on your students.

ACTION STEP #1: CELEBRATE GROWTH AND SUCCESS

I love to celebrate just as much as I love to set goals! So why not celebrate the little wins along the way? But really, why not? It is important to celebrate the attempts we have made in our work just as much as the end result. Many goals take time to achieve and require a great deal of effort. Without taking opportunities to reflect and celebrate the effort and growth throughout the process, we can easily lose sight of the purpose for our goals. The extensive time can make it harder to work for what we want to achieve, especially if it is far from our reach. Beginning teachers need help with this process in order to stay in the game of teaching. Really, so do we as mentors.

The learning process comes with chances, imperfection, and messiness as we take risks. Often the real learning takes place through failure. The defeat may not be fun to celebrate, but usually we learn from our failures and with encouragement, we try again. Eventually, we succeed, having grown in the process. This is where the need to celebrate big comes in! The importance of recognition extends to students, as children and teens are not accustomed to understanding the process it takes to grow.

MENTOR TIP

Use the Learning Mindset Progression from Chapter 3 to discuss ways of becoming an innovative thinker.

One idea to get you started as you collaborate with your mentee is to simply discuss a celebration so far in the day. Work with your mentee to brainstorm ideas for celebrating creative and critical thinking along the pathway to being an innovative thinker. Remember that finding solutions and seeking improvement are part of the work. Whether the goal is achieved or not, you can still have fun along the way. Here are some ideas for celebrating the learning mindset process that you and your mentee can add onto:

- You catch a mistake

- It doesn't go right the first time teaching a lesson

- You have to change your plan mid-lesson

- You ask a question

- You have tried something more than once and you keep trying

IN THE CLASSROOM

These celebration ideas can be used with students as well. Helping students understand persistence and flexibility are huge celebrations. Remind them that solutions and improvement are a key part of the hard work, even if a goal is not fully met.

ACTION STEP #2: REFLECT ON PRACTICES AND REVISE GOALS

An important part of the collaborative process is to work with your mentee to routinely reflect on their goals, teaching practices, and student impact. If you have already been meeting regularly with your mentee, you should build in designated time to periodically have these reflective conversations. Some mentors do these check-ins monthly. Another option is to do so mid-year. I work with a group of mentors and we have routinely built in collaborative work time to reflect on the first semester and set goals for the remainder of the year with mentees present. These collaborative work sessions are a highlight for the group, as it is time specifically meant to reflect together and hear from other mentor/mentee partnerships.

A great place to begin with reflecting on previous goals is to utilize the Learning Mindset Progression in Chapter 3. If you and your mentee did not have a goal-setting conversation yet, it is okay to reflect together on the work of the year thus far and set goals to work toward for the remainder of the school year. Another option is to utilize the directional supports to analyze progress and further needs. The key is to have communication about progress and make a plan for next steps.

The protocol in Figure 4.2 is a possible way to structure a collaborative goal reflection discussion with your mentee. A section of the protocol conversation is devoted to having your mentee share a moment or experience supportive of their passion for working with students. This helps to remind your mentee of their "why" and is important to collectively reflect together on how that keeps our passion alive. An additional idea could then be to relate back to your beliefs work.

Figure 4.2 Goal Reflection Inquiry Protocol

---

1. Celebrate and give thanks!

   • Have your mentee write a reflection about what has gone well so far this year.

   • Have your mentee write a thank you note or send an email to someone in the school that helped support them and their students.

   • Discuss the written reflection together and celebrate the success.

2. Recall your why!

   • Have your mentee think about a moment or experience that supported their passion for working with students. Discuss that together.

3. Set new goals

   • Review and discuss the directional supports

   • Use the ideas for support (shared in Chapter 2) to think about the areas to support growth.

   • Discuss and set a mentoring goal with an action plan for the remainder of the year, including at least one detail to attempt next week, next month, and the end of the year.

IN THE CLASSROOM

Designate time to be reflective about goals and progress with students as well. Embed opportunities for students to co-create learning targets and success criteria in order to motivate them to examine their own learning.

STRATEGY #2: REVISIT BELIEFS AND EQUITABLE EXPECTATIONS OF STUDENTS

Expectations connect back to our beliefs about learning and impact. For example, your mentee may have the perspective that their students will all magically learn and understand a skill the first time they teach a concept. Another common expectation is that they may expect to have enough time to teach what they planned. What does your mentee expect to be able to do as a teacher? You would hope they believe in their teaching potential and are consistently revisiting goals for how to best impact their students. How can a new teacher truly know unless they have more than one reflective conversation in a mentoring partnership? Let's consider the definitions of the term *expectation*, so you and your mentee can uncover your beliefs of students more thoroughly:

▶ Definition 1: A strong belief that something will happen or be the case in the future

▶ Definition 2: A belief that someone will or should achieve something

Source: Oxford Dictionary (2021)

Where does any new teacher expect to be at any point in their career? For some of our mentees, their view could be realistic in that they know it is tough but they are going to keep trying. Others may have an unrealistic view in that they either think or thought they should have it all together by now. I commonly hear, "I thought I could do all of these things, but now I realize the goal was too lofty." Mentees should have high expectations of themselves but will need to consistently revisit those goals with your help along the way. Also help them learn from their moments, both positive and negative. To visualize that correlation, let's revisit the balance between a fixed and innovator's mindset and replace "time" with "expectations" (Figure 4.3). There is a direct correlation to the importance of having higher expectations and growing our mindset about learning. If we expect more and are willing to take the time to learn, then we are more apt to be innovative and successful. With higher expectations come more fruitful results for both you and your mentee.

Figure 4.3 Learning Mindset and Expectation Tug-of-War

Think back to the communication support from the compass directions. A needs assessment going deeper into the beliefs around our expectations of impact could be another addition to one of your regular meetings (Figure 4.4). Notice the belief statements are from the Efficacy Beliefs Self-Reflection in Chapter 3, but the heading uses the language based on your current group of students or situation. The situation is more about the specific teaching role and setting. For example, when discussing the belief about having conversations with colleagues about student learning, what does the mentee think that will look like? Do they have a simplistic view of talking in passing as they go down the hall? Are they familiar with student problem-solving teams?

Figure 4.4 Needs Assessment on Expectations From Beliefs

Belief Statements	Based on My Current Group of Students or Situation, This Looks Like . . .
I believe all students have the ability to learn.	
I am confident I can motivate all students to learn.	
I am well prepared to teach the information I am assigned to teach.	
Learning takes place in my classroom because students are not worried about external factors in their home life.	
If a student in my classroom does not learn something the first time, we will try to find another way.	

Belief Statements	Based on My Current Group of Students or Situation, This Looks Like . . .
It takes a collaborative effort to positively impact student learning.	
I am willing to try new methods to better meet the needs of my students.	
It is important to have conversations with colleagues about student learning.	
I like to observe other classrooms in order to grow my repertoire of instructional strategies.	
I will ask for feedback from another colleague, instructional coach, principal, or students.	
I have developed ways to cope when a stressful situation arises with students.	
I balance my time working with students and self-care throughout my day.	

MENTOR TIP

Now that you have more of an idea about incorporating reflection of goals and progress, consider adding check-ins around expectations of beliefs as a part of that process. Embed the question, What do you expect students to do/learn as a result of your teaching?

Our judgments of students set our expectations and ultimately set our students up for success or failure. It is a teacher's estimate of their achievement. What does that mean? On Hattie's (2012) list of effect sizes, teacher estimates of achievement is at a 1.44 effect size. It is defined as

Teacher Estimates of Achievement: The estimates of student achievement made by teachers. These teacher judgments: can help set expectations; be used to benchmark past understanding; are involved in setting the next challenges, identify those who may have early signs of difficulties; inform placement and intervention choices; and influence instructional choices. These judgments come from questioning, observing, written work presentations, how the student reacts to increased challenge, and assignments and tests.

Source: Visible Learning MetaX (n.d.c)

It is mind blowing to know that what we estimate sets our expectations of students and can be such a huge factor in their achievement! That means you have some work to do in helping guide your mentee to having appropriately high expectations of all of their students. I would also add that this is where it is necessary to bring up the conversation related to our beliefs about students learning despite their home life. We have to put aside our bias and expect that all students can learn, hence the importance of always working toward being culturally responsive. Approaching this conversation may not come natural for you. Keep in mind how to use questioning in your conversations with your mentee that will push students further to believing in themselves. Here are some discussion questions you can ask mentees to promote equitable expectations:

> What do we envision our low and high expectation of learning should be?

> How can we push learners to go higher than their own expectation?

> Are we equitable when it comes to our expectations of students?

> What do we expect the student outcomes to be?

> How do we think all students will perform?

IN THE CLASSROOM

This also can be used with students, as they need to have higher expectations for themselves in order to be confident and open to learning. Student estimations of their own learning is not far off from reality. Interestingly enough, on the Visible Learning website, Hattie (Waack, 2021) shares that he would have named the strategy "Student Self-Reported Grades" as "Student Expectations." If students understand what is expected, they know if they are going to be successful when performing.

STRATEGY #3: PREPARE NEW TEACHERS BY SHARING ADDITIONAL EXPERIENCES

Our beliefs are built from experiences. Sharing our experiences is what helps humans connect and form stronger relationships. It also is an ongoing action to recount stories dependent on various moments throughout a year. Each day as I go into a teacher's lounge or as I walk out of a school building, the buzz consists of teachers describing an experience from their day. The discussions then open a doorway to collaborative reflection and allow conversations to be more inclusive of students and their learning. If you don't have the bank of experiences to share, scenarios could help you and your mentee as well.

ACTION STEP #1: BUILD ON EXPERIENCES TO GROW YOUR MENTEE'S REPERTOIRE

As a mentor, you can build on a beginning teacher's experiences by sharing what you have learned from your own teaching. We touched on this in Chapter 1 when we discussed those first few weeks of school. Now, your mentee is ready to take it the next level with their learning and reflection. Some of the times to consider are after winter break when you normally begin to see students changing. Or another monumental time is when mentees are preparing for conference updates with parents and caregivers.

Many teachers go through a memorable experience at some point. Some go through several! Adding more of your stories is yet another aspect that is significant to the mentoring relationship and jointly reflecting with mentees. Recall the experiences you have also added to your toolbox over the years that could be most relevant to your mentee. Some moments may easily pop out to you more than others. Think proactively as to what you may want to share that could be imperative to your mentee. How can you be proactive in knowing what experiences to share? If you are like me, how can you remember them all?! I recommend taking a trip down memory lane. Some of the ways I like to do that are by looking at my class profile pictures or trying the activity of going through a timeline of major events from past years. Try looking over the categories of directional support. Pay particular attention to the classroom management strategies you use and how those have played a part in how you have run your classroom in the past. You may also think about some of your curricular units previously taught. Particular activities or projects may stand out to you because of distinct experiences—either positive or challenging. They may be like the following pivotal ideas:

- Looking at class profile pictures

- Going through a timeline of major events from past years

- Recalling curricular units previously taught

- Analyzing big projects or activities

- Using the emotional, communication, physical and instructional categories

- Considering classroom management tips and strategies

- Remembering family interactions

You will also notice an important idea on the list for recalling pivotal experiences—family interactions. Outside of our interactions with colleagues and students, one of the more integral areas for you to consider is sharing about experiences with caregivers. Communicating with parents and family members is extremely important in supporting students' learning. Teachers along with guardians are both key players in the learning of children. Parental expectations have an effect size of 0.70 (Visible Learning MetaX, n.d.e). It is a must in your joint collaboration to explain your experiences of how to effectively communicate student learning with caregivers. My biggest advice to new teachers is to always think of ways to communicate with families proactively. As mentors, we may not even realize the actions we take that promote positive and effective family communication. When you share stories with your mentee, include these tips in preparation of proactive communication with caregivers:

- Positive phone calls

- Weekly newsletter

- Website and/or social media (in accordance with school guidelines)

- Attending school functions outside of normal school hours

- Field trips or class learning experiences with parents

> ## 💡 MENTOR TIP
>
> It is also helpful to think back to Chapter 3's big ideas about being culturally responsive. Encourage your mentee to be mindful of the various family units and challenges families may have. Follow those conversations up with discussing ways to promote family involvement that meets the needs of every family.

ACTION STEP #2: DISCUSS REAL-WORLD SCENARIOS

An addition to collaborative reflection is discussing scenarios with your mentee. Scenarios allow you to have more experiences to problem-solve with your mentee. Mentors have found this to be a purposeful activity that promotes being proactive rather than reactive. Your mentee is then more prepared going into their classroom. It also allows your mentee to feel more prepared for conversations with colleagues, especially administrators, and families. A simple protocol to guide you in that conversation is in Figure 4.5. The focus is about the various options for responding to situations, as problem-solution thinking will increase a beginning teacher's confidence in themselves. Many scenarios have multiple next steps or ways to work through solutions, but it is important to give choice to your mentee where appropriate. It is also valuable to discuss the wrong way to go about a problem. Embed this activity into your regular meetings in a way that makes sense to you and your mentee, like at the beginning of every month.

Figure 4.5 Scenario Protocol

1. Mentor/Mentee partnership choose a scenario.
2. Discuss specific details that could come about within the example.
3. Think about responses to these questions together:
   - What is the student need and/or issue?
   - What questions should be asked?
   - What individuals, strategies, and resources would you go to or use to support the student along with solving the problem?

Possibilities for scenario ideas can come from thinking of the directional supports (Figure 4.6). Brainstorm authentic possibilities by thinking of a timeline of events through the year and for when to bring them up proactively. Keep in mind the age-appropriate actions to take. Some examples are more relatable to elementary versus high school age students, so consider your mentee's group of students. It is most notable to reflect on our biases in response to some or even all of the instances. Look closely at some of the examples in the table and note that gender bias is common without even realizing it.

Figure 4.6 Scenario Examples Related to Directional Supports

How Do We Respond to . . . ?	
Emotional	1. Madison, a very capable yet unmotivated girl, misses school a lot. She also goes to the nurse often and is constantly complaining of headaches or stomach issues.
	2. A parent just discovers that their son Jack is being bullied, despite the emails you have sent for the past few months about occurrences at lunch and recess. The parent comes up to school demanding a meeting immediately.
	3. Allie's parents recently separated, and she is beginning to act out in class as well as in other locations around the school.
Communication	4. A student hasn't completed some assignments, all right in a row. She says she hasn't had enough time to despite the rest of the class being finished in class with the work. Parental support is usually limited with the student.
	5. Brock is new to the school and has an educational autism and ADHD diagnosis. He started the first month of school receiving writing services and was participating in the group successfully. Now, his behaviors have escalated to shouting out and being easily distracted.
	6. Keegan is on his phone again. When you nicely ask him to put the phone away, he tells you no and then purposely ignores you.
Physical	7. Students are leaving supplies and materials all over the classroom. The custodian has even asked for you to try not to leave such a mess.
	8. Meredith began showing signs of needing glasses, but upon talking with her, you realize that she also said she couldn't even see from the angle she sat in the room as you were teaching.
Instructional	9. Gabe is constantly asking you to check his work to make sure he is doing it correctly. It is taking time away from the whole class every day.
	10. Jay rarely turns in his homework and is failing, even though he consistently makes Cs on unit tests. When you ask him about the homework, he says he didn't think you would help him unless he was a girl.
	11. Katelyn is given a reading test and you notice the use of African American Vernacular English, or AAVE, when reading the fluency portion out loud.

Some example scenarios can fit into more than one category, which is perfectly acceptable, as there are different ways the actual event could play out. The examples given are only a small snippet of possible situations your mentee could encounter. Other areas to consider are planning, assessment, behavior, cultural responsiveness, and management. The power is in the discussion of potential actions and can be helpful to you as well as your mentee.

MENTOR TIP

Embed a scenario into your regular discussions with mentees to promote proactive problem solving.

STRATEGY #4: HELP NEW TEACHERS MAKE ADJUSTMENTS TO CLASSROOM MANAGEMENT AND STUDENT ENGAGEMENT

Setting up a classroom is a first-year teacher's dream, even before they get their first job. Rightfully so—if they want to have a functioning classroom, the layout of everything is important to plan out. We briefly mentioned arrangement in a tip in an earlier chapter. The importance of mentioning classroom set-up again is because it is connected to management and engagement, two areas that are the most important in beginning teacher professional development. Yet again, we want to go deeper in analyzing whether students are learning by considering the affects of management and engagement routines. You will also want to take your mentee through the steps of revision and try new options based on their student needs. You can start by asking, "What do you need to adjust to make sure students are engaged and learning?" To ease the stress, providing physical support from your end is necessary. Be careful as to not squash the excitement of a new teacher's vision.

MENTOR TIP

There are a plethora of ideas on classroom arrangement and organization tips. The key is in how to promote a student-centered environment that fosters a collective mindset and encompasses innovative learning. Take your mentee on a quick tour of other classrooms to help those areas.

Asking questions is one way to guide mentees toward how to evaluate the best options of a student-centered classroom:

▶ What arrangement of desks/tables/seats can I have that promotes dialogue over monologue?

▶ Where do I set up my teacher areas and technology tools to best utilize instructional time (as well as save me time)?

▶ How can I promote a welcoming and collaborative environment for learning?

▶ What tools and resources need to have spaces to promote student independence?

▶ What charts and visuals need to be given priority while also minimizing student distractions?

I would also review the brain-based learning resources mentioned in Chapter 3. Consider class make-up and promote a welcoming classroom that connects the look of a classroom to the cultures of the students. This is important in order to help students' perception that they are accepted as part of the classroom community and encourage their interest in being a collaborative learner, hence the connection to engagement. Since many first-year teacher programs consist of these areas, it is important for you to research the ideas they have been given. Either ask your mentee, administrator, or district mentor coordinator for that information to support and further the work. Just like with students, we can give new teachers too much information. It is also better to review the ideas so as not to overwhelm your mentee with an abundance of options.

IN THE CLASSROOM

Getting feedback from students is a piece of the puzzle that supports engagement. We are not just recommending how to give strengths-based feedback but observing and seeing the ways students react to engaging with and managing ideas. Some considerations are examining the attention getters and expectations. Then, see how students respond as well as elicit students' thoughts. Again, there are a multitude of ideas and ways to build a positive environment that utilizes effective techniques. Some new teachers may need to review steps with students or adjust with student input.

Another way to support these topics is to do an activity of reading about the key features of management and engagement. Then, discuss how the similarities and differences between the two compare. One of the most recent collaborative work sessions I participated in consisted of the mentor and mentee doing this work together with two articles. From that work, a mentor and mentee partnership came up with the idea of how relationships are at the center of both concepts! Other partnerships in sessions have completed visual representations from their collaboration. The results were powerful from the activity. See the examples of some of the work in Figure 4.7 to promote ideas with your mentee.

Figure 4.7 Engagement and Management Visual Representations

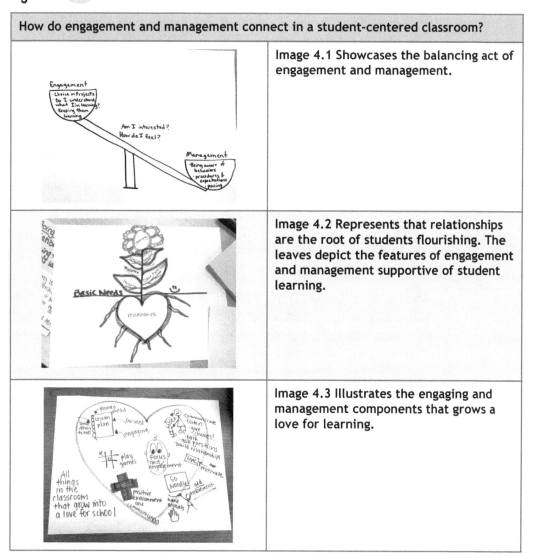

How do engagement and management connect in a student-centered classroom?	
	Image 4.1 Showcases the balancing act of engagement and management.
	Image 4.2 Represents that relationships are the root of students flourishing. The leaves depict the features of engagement and management supportive of student learning.
	Image 4.3 Illustrates the engaging and management components that grows a love for learning.

STRATEGY #5: INCORPORATE MORE DISCUSSION ABOUT YOUR MENTEE'S IMPACT

There will come a day for you to magnify the conversations about impact. When your mentee is ready to enhance their student-centered learning environment, you can employ these action steps. Strategy 1 focuses on gathering student evidence to support discussions with your mentee. Teena Pirkle has mentored multiple teachers and reiterates that, "The power of collaboration and helping each other remember strategies and practices that help our students more was so amazing from our partnership." This will help you and your mentee to dive into more formative assessment options and assist with planning next steps. The second action step will extend their reflection of solutions using collaborative inquiry. Many mentors realize they too can learn with their mentee, as many pick up little bits from their mentee.

ACTION STEP #1: COLLABORATE USING STUDENT EVIDENCE

Another of Hattie and Zierer's (2018) 10 Mindframes for Visible Learning is the following: "I collaborate with my peers and my students about my conceptions of progress and my impact." This mindframe supports the mentoring partnership as you and your mentee discuss how to share responsibilities with teammates and overcome failures together.

I have witnessed several partnerships that found the most success in their planning conversations when they centered their discussion on student evidence. Whether you look at concrete student data or observations, the conversations can follow a simple pattern. Starting with asking the question, What evidence will give us the full picture of student learning? Whether this is a pre-assessment of some kind or checkpoints along the way, gathering information is a necessary part of our job as teachers. Otherwise, we are teaching blindly and hoping students will catch something along the way. You will need to guide your mentee to take this approach in order for them to be most effective. This work directly connects to giving high quality lessons, which we will study further in Chapter 5. Take note of these collaborative planning steps using student evidence:

1. Discuss the student evidence needed.

2. Collect student evidence

3. Look for trends.

4. Identify student learning needs.

5. Decide next steps.

Student evidence not only drives our conversations around instructional planning but, more than anything, should drive the conversations about evaluating the impact we have on students. Essentially, help your mentee ask themself if all of their students are growing and learning. Then follow up with what can be adjusted in their instruction. Having conversations together to help model the thinking will best help students.

 KEEPING IT STUDENT CENTERED

You may be inclined to go straight toward planning using a particular teacher resource manual. Instead, try to collaborate with your mentee about using student evidence to assess their impact on learning before beginning the planning phase.

ACTION STEP #2: SET UP A COLLABORATIVE INQUIRY WITH YOUR MENTEE

What better opportunity is there to learn alongside a colleague than when it is a new teacher yearning to learn? One aspect of the mentoring partnership that tends to go by the wayside is collaboration around new learning ideas. There are two possibilities to learn together, and they are right under your nose. I recommend the use of the first option, which is a more advanced structure, when partnering with mentees in their second year of teaching or beyond. The second option is a modified version of the first procedure.

> ## MENTOR TIP
>
> Reentry teachers are also good candidates for partnering in a meaningful study using the Collaborative Inquiry Cycle. You can approach them with topics dependent on their student needs. Possible examples include using text evidence to support their reasoning, solving multi-digit multiplication problems in various ways, or developing a thesis statement with a counter argument.

Here is a structure that opens up the door to the inquiry of student evidence and capitalizes on the opportunity to further enhance your mentoring partnership. Jenni Donohoo (2013) gives us one option with the Collaborative Inquiry for Educators in stages. It is an in-depth process teams and partners can take when exploring student learning needs in their classroom and schools. I like to think of this option like a case study. The four stages are as follows:

1. **Frame the problem:** Determine a focus, develop an inquiry, and form a theory of action.

2. **Collect evidence:** Develop shared understanding, determine type of evidence and details of collection.

3. **Analyze the evidence:** Make meaning of the results and form conclusions.

4. **Document, share, and celebrate:** Consider new understandings and next steps.

Generally, teachers brand new to the profession are overwhelmed with already trying out so many new ideas as it is, so mentors may want to focus on an inquiry at least mid-year into the partnership, or after. Time constraints from induction and certification requirements will also need to be a priority. If your year-one mentee is still looking to inquire, try using a less intensive process. I suggest modifying the preceding process to a more simplistic structure (Figure 4.8). There are five steps that can be done based on your timeline. The example given is a common literacy example that would be inclusive of a beginning teacher's classroom. The process is based on the student learning needs in the new teacher's room and is essentially another way to think about problems and solutions. The student learning needs can be centered on engagement and management difficulties the first-year teacher may be experiencing. Similar to the scenario activities, the reflection is powerful and supportive of the impact we want to have on student learning.

Figure 4.8 Modified Collaborative Inquiry for Mentoring Partnership

Mentor Inquiry Steps With an Example	
1. Identify a student learning need	Students are struggling with choosing books to read and staying engaged during independent reading.
2. Develop a focused goal	Students will develop strategies for being an independent reader.
3. Complete a short inquiry	Review our guide to our reading resource and check in with reading specialists.
4. Decide 1–3 action steps	• Give students "look-fors" when picking out appropriate amounts of books and model the process. • Help students make a plan for their reading. • Rotate varied ideas for sharing about reading with a partner and whole-class debriefs.
5. Review end results and celebrate	• Students are taking less time to choose books and stamina has increased. • Students love sharing about their reading, and some have formed their own book clubs.

MENTOR TIP

If you feel your mentee is not quite ready for either of these areas, consider integrating an inquiry structure in the second year of your mentoring partnership to promote continued support.

FROM THE LENS OF A NEW TEACHER

How Natalie Transferred Collaborative Reflection to Other Partnerships

Natalie was a first-year mentee, fresh out of college. Rodney, her mentor, had also been her cooperating teacher the year prior for her student-teaching experience. Their partnership had already started

(Continued)

(Continued)

from a positive standpoint. Natalie was hired on when an opening came up for the following school year. Both Natalie and Rodney were first-grade teachers in a kindergarten through second-grade elementary. This meant that their grade-level team was larger than most, with about nine teachers, and Natalie had a multitude of people to go to if needed. Despite the large group, Natalie made sure her go-to person was her mentor, Rodney. Here's what Natalie shared about what she learned during her first year of teaching:

Just slow down! It is easy to get caught up in the day-to-day things to do for any teacher. Finding the time to have conversations about students with your mentor forces you to slow down and really think about your impact on students' learning. As you talk about particular students' data, whether observational or student results, it leads to being more mindful about progress, needs and next steps.

As a first-year teacher, you just don't know. I was nervous to ask questions, and I had a lot. I remember in the beginning prepping for our mentor conversations thinking: I want to ask about this student. . . . I want to ask about this resource. . . . I want to ask about this school event. . . . I want to ask about how to give a certain assessment. . . . I was all over the board! The power was when we honed in on students in our conversations.
I began to wonder most about if my kids were growing in reading. I started asking more questions about particular students, students who were not only below, but also those who were on the bubble with their reading levels. Where are students at now? Where are they struggling? Where do I go next with this student? Unfortunately, it was students who I knew did not qualify for intervention services. I'll never forget specifically wondering: How do we even get them from a Guided Reading level C to a D? All of these wonders also led to other questions. Most importantly, how do I keep my kids engaged in reading when I can't meet with them or work with them in a small group?

Plan time goes by in a snap, but my mentor helped me to see the importance of prioritizing the most impactful things during our time together. We purposefully spent time analyzing data and my students over some of the other "things." We were originally required to meet regularly with our mentor, but we found a routine of meeting more often than required because my mentor also helped me see the purpose—discussing impact on students is what makes the impact. Checking in became natural for us, and we would have in-depth conversations around students at least a few times a week. Again, slowing down and really understanding the effect I was having on my students' progress. Those supportive conversations led my mentor to guide me to seek out other people for help when I had questions, too. The entire process made me more comfortable to talk about instructional practices. Looking back, slowing down is what I needed for those student problem-solving sessions to help me make that impact. Best lesson learned: Question until you know, not fake it until you make it!

Natalie's description of aspects from their mentoring partnership highlights the importance of focusing on student-centered conversations to encourage a collective mindset. This shift in focus led to the two of them going deeper into the layers of Student-Centered Mentoring. Some of Natalie's other favorite memories for her first year were peer observations. Read more about her experience with peer observations in Chapter 5 and her experience with participating in a Mentor Coaching Cycle with Rodney and their literacy coach in Chapter 6.

MENTOR TIP

Share this Lens of a Mentee experience with your mentee and highlight the lesson learned: Question until you know, not fake it until you make it!

FROM THE LENS OF A MENTOR

How Rodney Modeled Evidence-Based Thinking to Make Instructional Decisions

How many of you are wondering about the view of the collaboration from Natalie's mentor, Rodney? Well, you are in luck because it is fitting that we hear from Rodney's perspective on their mentoring partnership. Rodney is excited and proud to share that he was a supervising teacher as well as mentor for Natalie. Rodney likes to add that he almost passed up the opportunity and declined the first request. Their relationship was positive from that student teaching experience, and it only made sense for the duo to be matched up

(Continued)

(Continued)

again when Natalie was hired on the team the following year. He looks back on how everything always plays out the way it does for a reason and gives his account of their work together:

I like to pay it forward in life. I have always known I wanted to be a mentor and to do the very same thing that someone did for me when I was a beginning teacher. As a mentor, the biggest part of our job is to guide the protégé, as I liked to call Natalie. I learned to use my own experiences to help Natalie when she needed that guidance. I wanted to be sure to inspire her and luckily, I found she was similar in personality to me. I have always tried to maintain being open-minded and she also has an openness to ideas that was helpful in her beginning years. That particular characteristic is what's important for any teacher. It allowed both Natalie and me to be learners and jump right into trying strategies to help our students together.

Your role as a mentor is to use your experiences to be the voice of reason. More than anything, I believe our work is about the students. In our mentoring partnership, we are a sounding board and set the example to always be on the side of students, to be with them along their learning journey. I remember sharing my parent-teacher conference experience with Natalie and how the small gesture of sitting on the same side of the table as parents, showcased my belief with them as well. I told her I learned to sit on the same side of the table when meeting with them to show we are in it together to help their child grow. It goes a long way in our work to do just that. Sharing stories of how parents appreciate that gesture makes a bigger impact than we realize on the connections we make with students.

But, I learned just as much from her as I believe she did from me. She may not realize just how much. I still use her call and response with students, "Have a seat, take a load off your feet." And the students then respond, "Thank you, don't mind if I do." That is one of many ideas she taught me. She always told me I should give myself more credit for the passion I have with being right there with the kids. Really, her passion for helping students is what's contagious to me. Luckily, I get to continue to teach with her and I feel like I am still responsible for mentoring Natalie in a way. Especially with highlighting her strengths—she is a great leader and should teach others from her experiences as well.

Rodney and Natalie continue to work on the same grade level, and their partnership today is still as strong as ever. He was a model of a mentor and passed the baton onto Natalie to mentor a teammate as well. Having the mindset that we inspire each other to be better every day is a result of the value of working collaboratively. Their mentoring partnership showcased that importance. It also helps to promote further learning, such as participating in learning labs alongside each other or a coaching cycle together. The duo did a mentor cycle in the second half of Natalie's first year, which is discussed in Chapter 6, if you want more details.

MENTOR TIP

Consider Rodney's view of what your mentoring role could be as well—to use your experiences to be the voice of reason for your protégé.

RECAP AND REFLECT

The goodness we discover from working together helps us follow our passion for educating students. Promoting a reflective mentality that is based on celebrating hard work and goal setting supports new teachers as they persevere through their beginning years. The role we play as mentors is to guide that process as well as showcase the importance of revising our goals and plans. The work does not stop there, as we revisit our belief system and revise expectations to be relevant to all students. We can also build our repertoire of experiences through thinking proactively by collaborating around potential scenarios. Our mentoring effort continues as we strive to learn more through an inquiry process that we can do alongside our mentees. The strength of the collective partnership is based on the reflective conversations throughout your time together and provides support for both of you as you peel back the layers of Student-Centered Mentoring.

MENTOR INQUIRY REFLECTION

Think back to the guiding questions at the beginning of the chapter. Take some time to reflect on the questions that follow as well as use the Rubric for Student-Centered Mentoring Section #4 to help set goals and make a plan for yourself (Figure 4.9).

1. How can you embed celebration and reflection of progress into your mentoring conversations?

2. What are your expectations of your mentoring partnership? What are your general expectations of students?

3. How can you share your experiences and scenarios as you have collaborative discussions with your mentee?

4. Which Student-Centered Mentoring success criteria would you choose to support your mentoring partnership?

5. What are some initial action steps you can take to promote collaborative conversations with your mentee?

Figure 4.9 Rubric for Student-Centered Mentoring

#4: Engage in Collaborative Conversations About Impact on Students		
Beginner	Emerging	Innovative
The mentor is attempting to have reflective conversations, but the discussions are not grounded in (or guided by) student evidence.	The mentor promotes having reflective conversations with his/her mentee, at times guided by student evidence. These discussions might also consist of problem solving how to increase student-learning opportunities.	The mentor takes part in routinely having collaborative conversations using student evidence. These discussions are reflective of how changes in instructional practices impact students' learning.

Success Criteria

- I can encourage discussions around real-world scenarios.
- I can reflect with my mentee and assist in setting goals to propel student learning forward.
- I can model how to evaluate my impact on student learning.
- I can showcase inquiry thinking around instructional practices.

LEARNING TOGETHER IN THE CLASSROOM

Strategies for Incorporating Observational Learning Opportunities

Strategy #1: Establish Observation Look-Fors
to Support Effective Pedagogy

> Action Step #1: Make Effective Instructional
> Strategies Clear to New Teachers
>
> Action Step #2: Create Observation Goals and Look-Fors

Strategy #2: Guide New Teachers in Observing
in-the-Moment Assessment Options

Strategy #3: Embed Observational Learning Methods
Into Your Mentoring Partnership

> Action Step #1: Prepare for Peer Observations
>
> Action Step #2: Participate in a Mentee/Mentor Learning Lab

Strategy #4: Implement the Strategies Observed With Support

> Action Step #1: Promote Positive Pressure
>
> Action Step #2: Help Each Other Remain Accountable

All teachers visualize having a highly creative and facilitated activity where student learning is off the charts. First year teachers, like Lauren Gill, dream of that moment. Lauren took the opportunity to learn from other teachers to achieve that dream herself. She was hooked after her first observation experience and walked away with an abundance of takeaways. She recalls learning instructional strategies from a teacher whose teaching style was different from her own, yet she had a similar classroom of students. Lauren shares, "I remember how Katie sang songs to engage the students and explained why she incorporated music throughout her lesson." Along with her mentor, Lauren has continued to attend other learning labs and observe other teachers to grow her instructional understanding. The duo gained many ideas and strategies, both from their own observations and from the debrief sessions after their time in classrooms. Lauren excitedly sums up her reflection of these moments, "We took all the wonderful things we learned from students and the host teacher, and then tried them in our own classrooms."

Learning alongside mentees is the best way to engage everyone in the learning process. "Tell me and I forget, teach me and I may remember, involve me and I learn" said philosopher Xun Kuang (as cited on Goodreads, 2021). It is time to take the next step in working with beginning teachers. You will want to embed more about practices and teaching strategies in your mentoring conversations to boost your mentee's instructional clarity. Lead your mentee through observational processes, which are significant to transferring the learning of effective practices, increasing your mentee's capacity, and building their confidence in teaching. You can do this by arranging learning labs and peer observations with a specific eye on student learning. Mentors have the option to help organize or jump in on observational opportunities as well. This leads to the third section of the layers of Student-Centered Mentoring (Figure 5.1): observational learning.

Figure 5.1 Layers of Student-Centered Mentoring With Key Ideas

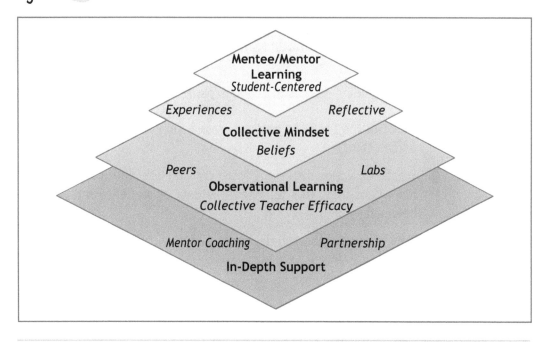

WHAT IS THIS CHAPTER ABOUT?

In this chapter, you will learn strategies to

- Cultivate effective instructional pedagogy with your mentee

- Embed observational learning methods into your mentoring experience

- Increase implementation of student-centered instructional practices

This chapter will explore how it is all encompassing of these observational opportunities for you and your mentee to learn together in the classroom. This third layer supports the direction of a mentee's instructional needs. We get to the meat of teaching when we discuss providing instructional support for new teachers. This chapter will also showcase how observational learning can promote collective teacher efficacy in your school. A major plus to the mentoring partnership is that both of you benefit from a student-centered focus as you view the work of other classrooms in varied ways. Observational learning also promotes positive pressure and gives you ways to follow up on the experiences in order to help hold each other accountable in trying out the ideas with students.

MENTOR INQUIRY PRE-REFLECTION

Use these guiding questions as you explore the ideas in this chapter:

1. How can you promote positive pressure in your mentoring partnership?

2. What instructional strategy focus can you help your mentee identify as they work to increase impact on students in their beginning years?

3. How can you embed student-centered observations into your work with your mentee?

WHAT IS THE SIGNIFICANCE OF CLASSROOM OBSERVATIONS?

In all of my work with new teachers, one of the experiences they ask for the most is to observe other teachers in action. This accounts for mentee's visual understanding of how to impact students the most and is another way to foster collective teacher efficacy. As Jenni Donohoo (2017) says, "Collective teacher efficacy is enhanced when teams of educators observe success in school environments similar to their own." For new teachers, observations usually start with you, their mentor. If you are in the same content area or grade level, this is a perfect place to start observations. If not, try to embed observation opportunities for your mentee that include the familiarity of their own classroom. I have found it to be most helpful to arrange the first observation for new teachers to see the same age of students they service. After your mentee observes a host teacher in the same age group, you can help arrange other observations.

Classroom observations are also important to support your mentee's growth. The host teacher you choose should be able to demonstrate something that can help meet your mentee's most pressing needs first. Think about the directional supports and consider if a connection can be made to something specific, like communication or physical support. The top priorities for many beginning teachers are the areas of classroom management and relationships, which typically connect to the programs they go through for the first-year continuing certifications. Another common priority is promoting a culturally responsive classroom. Rather than just having the mentee watch, talk about what they should look for using the focus as guidance to give your mentee purpose. Then, work with your mentee to balance observation options that include the familiarity of their own classroom, as well as other classroom types. The following strategies will help you plan and prepare new teachers for successful observations.

MENTOR TIP

Prepare for any observation beforehand and have a pre-observation meeting with the host teacher. You want to reassure the host teacher that the mentee's need is to see real teaching. Set the tone that it is a moment of learning for your mentee and if something has to be changed on the spot during instruction, then even better! It will give the mentee opportunity to see how flexible teachers have to be during their lessons.

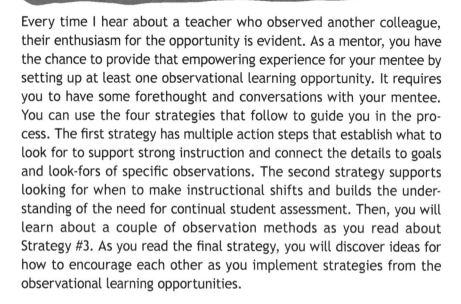

STRATEGIES FOR INCORPORATING OBSERVATIONAL LEARNING OPPORTUNITIES

Every time I hear about a teacher who observed another colleague, their enthusiasm for the opportunity is evident. As a mentor, you have the chance to provide that empowering experience for your mentee by setting up at least one observational learning opportunity. It requires you to have some forethought and conversations with your mentee. You can use the four strategies that follow to guide you in the process. The first strategy has multiple action steps that establish what to look for to support strong instruction and connect the details to goals and look-fors of specific observations. The second strategy supports looking for when to make instructional shifts and builds the understanding of the need for continual student assessment. Then, you will learn about a couple of observation methods as you read about Strategy #3. As you read the final strategy, you will discover ideas for how to encourage each other as you implement strategies from the observational learning opportunities.

STRATEGY #1: ESTABLISH OBSERVATION LOOK-FORS TO SUPPORT EFFECTIVE PEDAGOGY

It is a two-step process to help mentees remain focused during observations. First, mentees need to be clear on how to identify instructional strategies. Then, mentees can use the knowledge of specific strategies to guide their goal setting and hopes for takeaways from the observation. We do this work so that they can take back what they have learned and adjust their own practices. Traditionally, content is the focus of observational learning, as it is often most needed for new teachers. But we can't forget the *how* in teaching that content. Having a clear understanding of effective instruction and using that knowledge to guide observation look-fors will support your mentee in a more profitable observation experience.

ACTION STEP #1: MAKE EFFECTIVE INSTRUCTIONAL STRATEGIES CLEAR TO NEW TEACHERS

As a mentor, you can help guide beginning teachers to have a clearer understanding of using and seeing effective instructional strategies with students by turning your mentoring conversations toward instructional strategies that are student centered. In Chapter 3, there is a protocol to help new teachers analyze the Visible Learning Strategies and use them to narrow in on the domains of student learning. If your mentee have chosen to work with a few of those areas, keep those in mind when discussing strategies during observation planning meetings with your mentee. Just be sure everyone understands what the specific strategy really means! Use these questions to define and visualize instructional strategies with your mentee:

> What does the strategy really mean?

> What is the purpose of the strategy?

> How does it look in the classroom?

As you think about ways to guide your mentee, I bet you are already visualizing student success in the classroom. There are several aspects within instruction, and it is extremely difficult to pick just one strategy or practice that may be more important and most effective, especially as a beginning teacher. The strategy that makes the most sense is an umbrella to all other strategies: teacher clarity.

> **Teacher clarity:** relates to organization, explanation, examples and guided practice, and assessment of student learning. It can involve clearly communicating the intentions of the lessons and the success criteria. Clear learning intentions describe the skills, knowledge, attitudes, and values that the student needs to learn. (Visible Learning MetaX, n.d.d)

How do you determine if clarity of learning is being achieved? In line with my love of questions comes the clear pathway to help learners achieve this—ask students questions! Almarode and Vandas (2018) give these three questions as options to ask students:

- What are you learning?

- Why are you learning it?

- How will you know if you've learned it?

In their book *Clarity for Learning*, Almarode and Vandas (2018) outline the importance of clarity in teaching and learning, as it serves as the foundation for all other significant influences to be possible. For a new teacher—or you might even be thinking of yourself—attaining teacher clarity may seem like a daunting task. I have narrowed it down to a few areas you can first look at closer (Figure 5.2). This is where your role comes in—collaborating with your mentee to identify the most appropriate one to start with. Think of your mentee's instructional needs and style of teaching. Of course, always encourage thinking in connection to student-centered instruction. If they all seem like a good match, tackle one at a time! Knowing what each is and what it looks like in the classroom is key to success as you talk about teaching and student learning with your mentee.

When your mentee is ready to include more of the Visible Learning Strategies, you might be inclined to focus on the highest effect sizes. Instead, consider the connection that many of the strategies have with each other and choose strategies that connect with your mentee's prior focus. To do this, look closely at the sub-domain categories of student-learning strategies or teaching strategies. It will be beneficial to use any of these as a focus when observing other classrooms, which we will break down further in the next step.

Figure 5.2 Effective Instructional Strategies With a Student-Centered Lens

	What is it?	What is the purpose?	What does it look like in a student-centered classroom?
Learning Intentions and Success Criteria	Intended learning outcomes and evidence to achieve intentions	Gives students direction and logical progression for learning	• Clear goals and objectives • Demonstration of learning a skill/strategy • Modeled examples • Learning progressions • Promotes relevance
Feedback	Information that allows a learner to reduce the gap of current understanding to what could or should be understood	Highlights progress and reduces discrepancies of understanding	• Provided by teacher, peer, book, parent, self/experience • Strengths-based • Classroom discussion • Assessment-capable learners

Assessment	Checking for student understanding throughout the learning process	Look for patterns of students' learning to decide next steps and adjust teaching as needed	• How can students answer the following:
			  ○ Where am I going?
			  ○ How am I going (or doing)?
			  ○ Where do I go next?
			• Formal or informal
			• Observational
			• Written summative or end-of-course/unit methods
			• Alternative methods: oral presentations, progress monitoring, and performance methods

Adapted from: Almarode and Vandas (2018), Fisher and Frey (2019), Visible Learning MetaX (n.d.d)

MENTOR TIP

Work with your mentee to decide which instructional strategies should be a focus as you turn your attention to analyzing instruction. Make sure to keep the strategies in mind when helping your mentee plan their own instruction.

ACTION STEP #2: CREATE OBSERVATION GOALS AND LOOK-FORS

Ultimately, the goal of any learning lab or observation is to increase the clarity of learning for your mentee. The key is how to make that happen. As a mentor, it is important to consider all observation aspects in order to guide your mentee to gaining new knowledge they can actually implement in their own classroom. The following details are helpful as you prepare your mentee for an observation:

- goals
- look-fors
- effective practices
- alignment to induction work
- note-taking options

Wow! That is a hefty list, but it is possible to do by keeping in mind the stage your mentee is in with the beginning teacher process. Also, consider your mentee's directional support needs. Figure 5.3 has examples of mentor/mentee observation goals and look-fors that are supportive for peer observations or learning labs.

Figure 5.3 Examples of Mentor/Mentee Observation Goals and Look-Fors

	Learning Lab	Observation

Year 1 Mentee	• Teachers will develop understanding around maintaining relationships with students and colleagues.
	   ○ What students are doing and saying that connects to a positive classroom environment
	• Teachers will determine practices for student engagement throughout the workshop.
	   ○ How students are engaged throughout the workshop during conferring and small groups
		• Establishing management and structures that support student learning and independence.
		• Lesson parts (connection, teaching, active engagement, link)
		• Partner or group time
		• Debrief or share
		• Routines and behaviors
		• Modeled examples
		• Charts or signals

(Continued)

(Continued)

	Learning Lab	Observation

Year 2 Mentee	• Teachers will determine practices for using data to drive instruction.
	
	  ○ Ways students are giving formative assessment options to teachers (e.g., exit slips or non-paper/pencil options)
	
	  ○ How the students are tracking their own data
	
	• Teachers will develop understanding around maintaining relationships with students and colleagues.
	
	  ○ What students are doing and saying connecting to positive classroom community and relationships
		• Promoting critical thinking through classroom discussion opportunities
		• Student dialogue opportunities
		• Open-ended questioning by teachers and students
		• Frequency of students sharing
		• Level of student discourse
		• Student goal-setting and tracking of progress

As you look the examples over, notice the student learning within the goals for participants along with how you can highlight best practices in the look-fors. Also, keep in mind how you incorporate ways to connect back to relationships and being culturally responsive. Lastly, some of you may be unsure of the alignment to the mentee's induction program through your own school or district.

The examples in Figure 5.5 are based on the following typical new teacher program and district goal areas:

▶ **Year 1 Mentees:** Relationship focus and engagement

▶ **Year 2 Mentees:** Continuing relationship focus along with data and assessment

If these goals do not align with your school or districts main focus areas, look into the main topics of your new teacher induction program with your mentee and build off of that work. Another possibility is to simply have your mentee reflect on some of the key takeaways in their learning from their professional development sessions most states require. No matter what you decide, brainstorm the goals and look-fors together.

MENTOR TIP

Assist your mentee in coming up with goals and look-fors to guide any observation experience by asking questions related to goals, look-fors, effective practices, and their induction topics. Don't forget to share these pieces with the host teacher.

STRATEGY #2: GUIDE NEW TEACHERS IN OBSERVING IN-THE-MOMENT ASSESSMENT OPTIONS

In many teachers' classrooms, being clear on what to teach is coupled with also knowing when to adjust instruction. That trend connects to one of the categories for teacher clarity: assessment. The cause-and-effect relationship of teaching and assessing is a teacher needing to be clear on what student learning looks like and then checking for understanding of that learning. When it comes to planning instruction, most teachers assume what students already know and jump right into teaching students a concept or skill. More and more research shows that the majority of what students are being taught is information they have already mastered. John Hattie (2020) claims that this number is as high as 80%! This is where learning to assess can come in handy for beginning teachers. Helping your mentee understand the purpose of pre-assessing is an effective practice to guide the start of a unit or course. Your mentee will have a better view of the student learning intentions in an observation if this information is shared during a pre-brief of an observation.

KEEPING IT STUDENT CENTERED

You may be drawn to placing a heavy emphasis on using data from school-wide progress monitoring and yearly assessments. Rather than using that data, balance the data conversations with unit and classroom formative assessments as well. Encourage your mentee to plan lessons based on a quick pre-assessment or informal observations so they are clear on what to teach students. Couple that with prepping a few questions to check for understanding, so your mentee knows when to adjust instruction in the moment.

The next piece of assessment is to know when to change direction during a lesson or activity. As the authors mention in *The Teacher Clarity Playbook*, without processes, checking for understanding has the potential to be a game of "Guess What's in the Teacher's Brain" (Fisher et al., 2019). Getting feedback from students using various methods yields deeper understanding for teachers and students. For a new teacher, to see this work in the moment will be imperative to their instructional impact. During the debrief meeting with the host teacher of an observation, ask if there were moments where they veered from their original plan and why they made that decision. Mentees will benefit from hearing the thinking aloud.

One process option is questioning. If you really want true feedback from students, it comes down to the questions you ask—we have to make sure that the questions asked can give the information needed to make intentional and purposeful next steps. Those questions can be as simple as the ones noted in the assessment category in Figure 5.4. A new teacher can also reflect on their own questioning during lessons and activities. This process has shown to not feel overly cumbersome to new teachers. I highly suggest spending those few minutes with your mentee to figure out how to ask strategic questions that will yield what the majority of students already know or what they are picking up throughout a lesson or activity. Student engagement will likely go up along with achievement as well as the confidence of your mentee.

MENTOR TIP

You should also be transparent with your mentee and share when you change your course in a lesson or activity based on student responses.

STRATEGY #3: EMBED OBSERVATIONAL LEARNING METHODS INTO YOUR MENTORING PARTNERSHIP

It is finally time for your mentee to actually observe other educators. The first two strategies gave you the tools to set up these observations successfully. Now you can incorporate peer observations or learn alongside your mentee in a learning lab. Whether you choose one of these methods or have a varied compilation of them, you and your mentee will grow your mentoring partnership by adding these into your experience.

ACTION STEP #1: PREPARE FOR PEER OBSERVATIONS

Peer observations are one option for you to help your mentee set up. They are exactly as they are termed, observations of other colleagues and their classroom of students. This can even include your mentee observing your classroom as one of those peers. The first component to consider is when and how to structure the observations. Encourage your mentee to observe peers either during the mentee's plan time or work with your administrators to get sub coverage for a 15-30 minute time slot. Any amount of time will give your mentee ideas! If your mentee is lucky enough to have a sub for half a day, this provides a perfect opportunity to set up multiple observations in rounds. This is where you can take several approaches and even make it like a learning walk of sorts (Figure 5.4). Consider the approaches of three teachers on the same grade level; a vertical group of teachers or a cluster of teachers based around a common subject theme.

Figure 5.4 Peer Observation Round Examples

Examples of Peer Observation Rounds at Varying Levels		
	Focus Area and Trends to Observe	Teacher/Time and Subject
Primary Teacher	Main focus: Supporting students in reading and phonics Additional focus: Supporting struggling students	• **Teacher 1:** Mentor (20 minutes); phonics lesson and activity • **Teacher 2:** Grade-level teammate (30 minutes); reading small groups • **Teacher 3:** Reading interventionist (30 minutes); reading intervention pullout with struggling students
Upper Elementary Teacher	Main focus: Promoting student engagement through lesson structures	• **Teacher 1:** Prior grade level (15 minutes); writing lesson • **Teacher 2:** Mentor (15 minutes); math lesson • **Teacher 3:** Next grade level (15 minutes); reading lesson
Secondary Teacher	Main focus: Asking open-ended questions to stimulate students' critical thinking	• **Teacher 1:** Mentor (30 minutes); biology lesson • **Teacher 2:** Prior grade span (30 minutes); math lesson

> **MENTOR TIP**
>
> Model how to be a learner by going on your own peer observation and describing that experience to your mentee. Then, help your mentee set up peer observations of you and other colleagues. Be sure to share the student-centered observational focus with all host teachers.

The qualities that set apart peer observations as a Student-Centered Mentoring option from being teacher-centered is the lens of the mentee when observing. You will notice with the peer observation round examples that there is an area or trend to keep in mind for the mentee. Each one is similarly based on the student-learning piece. It is also important to set a focus area so as to not overwhelm your mentee when going into multiple classrooms. Another aspect of the peer observation is note-taking that includes the attention on students and the focus area. Figure 5.5 and 5.6 are a few options for you to recommend to your mentee. These are important for the two of you to then refer back to as you debrief the learning opportunity. Debriefing will be helpful to you as well, as you will pick up on ideas to transfer into your own practices.

Figure 5.5 Mentee Peer Observation Note Sheet #1

Focus		
Room 1	Room 2	Room 3
Student Evidence	Student Evidence	Student Evidence
Instructional Moves	Instructional Moves	Instructional Moves
Questions	Questions	Questions

Figure 5.6 Mentee Peer Observation Note Sheet #2

Focus		
	What do you notice the student(s) doing?	**How do you see the teacher respond to student(s)?**
Room 1		
	Questions	
Room 2		
	Questions	

![icon of three people]

KEEPING IT STUDENT CENTERED

The host teacher(s) or possibly you may be nervous about the mentee watching you teach a perfect lesson or activity. It will ease the host teacher's apprehension to have the note-taking tool geared toward students as well as provide your mentee with a visual of what to look for with their own students.

ACTION STEP #2: PARTICIPATE IN A MENTEE/MENTOR LEARNING LAB

Learning labs are an observation option that include a structure for a mentoring partnership or a group of mentors and mentees. I invite you to take on being a participant in this type of learning, as it is a way to have more of a shared experience with your mentee. In the work that I have done, all of the mentees and mentors who have participated in learning labs have walked away with increased teacher clarity as well as growth in their mentoring relationship. Even mentors have explained how much they love the time together and learn just as much, if not more, than their mentee. If you recall Kala, a mentor who shared her mentee story in Chapter 2, went on to participate in a mentee/mentor learning lab with Hannah.

> *We were able to digest the new learning together and try to find ways to add to what we are already doing. She was worried that she wasn't doing all of the same things that we saw. It was important for me to share in that moment with her because I could explain, "We all do things differently and make them our own." It was a way for both of us to get fresh ideas while still being who we were as teachers.*
>
> —Kala, Mentor

To grow your understanding of learning labs, you will find it helpful to obtain some background about them first. The concept of a learning lab has been built upon in the district I have worked in for many years alongside my District Instructional Coach Margo Mann. Our ideas have adapted through the research and work of Diane Sweeney. Three types of learning lab observations are explained in Diane's earlier work and provide the basis of understanding from generations of learning labs (Sweeney, 2011):

- Model classrooms
- Peer learning labs
- Student-centered labs

A fourth type of learning lab, mentor/mentee learning labs, grew as a result of my coaching experiences melding the other three together using a student-centered focus. As I worked with my director of professional development in Wentzville, Karen Hill, she allowed me to try mentee/mentor learning labs, which is how they grew into what they are today. Ultimately, that process included new teachers and mentors attending observations together, with their attention being primarily on students. In Figure 5.7, a comparison of the qualities is described for each of the four types.

Figure 5.7 Comparisons of Learning Lab Qualities

Types of Learning Labs	
Model Classrooms	• Teacher-centered learning lab based around current educational practices. • Observations are focused on how the host teacher goes about the business of teaching. • Lab host teacher is a confident, thoughtful, research-based and passionate teacher.
Peer Learning Labs	• Collaborative learning labs are based around questions of how to improve teacher learning that would therefore impact student learning. • Observations are focused on a question that is provided by the lab host teacher and are about the potential challenges of teaching and learning through a protocol that provides a safe environment. • Lab host teacher is selected not based on expertise but rather learning and reflection.
Student-Centered Labs	• Student-centered learning labs are based around a lens of student evidence to uncover ideas. • Observations are focused on a question posed by the host teacher along with student look-fors using a protocol and note-taking. • Lab host teacher volunteers to get feedback based on the collection of student evidence connected to a specific goal for students.
Mentee/ Mentor Labs	• Mentor and mentee learning labs are also based around a lens of student evidence to uncover ideas aligned with new teacher needs. • Observations are focused on foundational needs for new teachers with student look-fors using a protocol and note-taking. • Labs host teacher volunteers to showcase the reflection of feedback based on the collection of student evidence. • Mentee and mentor partners both attend to be a part of the learning together.

Adapted from Sweeney (2011)

 KEEPING IT STUDENT CENTERED

Embed an essential question in relation to student outcomes to guide the focus and the thinking of you and your mentee. You can also think ahead to the debrief or ask the facilitator for a question from there to make the learning come full circle.

The last step in incorporating learning labs with your mentee is to always have a structured protocol. The three-step basic structure of pre-brief, observe, and debrief is the way to make the most impact and use time wisely (Figure 5.8). It is a protocol you can include with any observation but especially for a learning lab experience that has more than your mentor partnership as participants. Times for each portion of the learning lab would just be longer than peer observations. Whether you are able to ask for this type of method to be used in your school or district or you use the pieces to create an experience just for your mentee, the protocol will be extremely useful in guiding you through the process.

Figure 5.8 Protocol for Mentee/Mentor Student-Centered Learning Lab

Mentee/Mentor Learning Lab With Student-Centered Focus	
Pre-brief with host teacher and participants (30-45 minutes)	• The facilitator will discuss norms for the observation and student learning "look-fors" to guide the debrief. • Host teacher will provide background information and the context for the work she is doing with students. **Norms** • Silence is golden in the classroom—honor the existing tone, structure, and community. Side conversations can be very distracting to everyone in the classroom and can upset the carefully developed learning environment. • It's not our turn to teach—you are a visitor in the classroom. Please do not engage with the students as a teacher. • Come with a positive attitude and be a learner—we are not here to critique the teacher. • Maintain focus—keep the look-fors in mind during observation. • Be ready to think through the entire process. • Take notes—bring your recorded student observations back to the debriefing session to support the conversation.
Observe learning (45-60 minutes)	• Observers take notes to share during the debriefing session. • Use a note-taking tool that is based around noticings of student learning and response to instructional practices. • Observers practice the norms discussed in the pre-brief meeting.

Mentee/Mentor Learning Lab With Student-Centered Focus	
Debrief in rounds (45-60 minutes)	• The group debriefs in rounds while the host teacher sits silent, listening is the gift of spying in on student learning.
	• Participants share as a "whip-around" to move the discussion along and can pass if needed.
	• If it is a group of participants, the facilitator summarizes and/or charts the round, capturing important themes and ideas.
	Rounds
	• What did you see students doing, in terms of tracking their own goals and applying/practicing the critical thinking skills they learn during reading/writing? (I noticed . . . I saw . . .)
	• What instructional practices did you see that impacted student learning? (I noticed . . . I saw . . . and because of this . . . students . . .)
	• Wonderings (I noticed . . . So, I wonder . . .)
	• Response from host teacher to wonderings.
	• Next steps—reflecting and thinking about next steps.

Adapted from Sweeney (2011)

MENTOR TIP

A first step is to look for opportunities where learning labs may be offered in your school or district. If none are available, ask a teammate or another colleague to host you and your mentee together.

STRATEGY #4: IMPLEMENT THE STRATEGIES OBSERVED WITH SUPPORT

How many times have you wished to try something you learned following an observation or professional learning experience? It is possible you forgot to try your new learning or never got around to giving something a go. In order to make the transfer of learning into a habit, you have to install some follow-up to your learning. As a mentor, it is your job to also help your mentee with that practice. Your mentoring partnership can provide the positive pressure and accountability needed to make that happen. These action steps will help you to empower your mentee as well as yourself in growing your instructional expertise.

ACTION STEP #1: PROMOTE POSITIVE PRESSURE

Pressure is naturally a part of the change process, and it is tricky to find pressure that is positive in helping move teacher and student learning forward (Sweeney, 2015). Teachers are under immense pressure as they wear many hats in their role. As we have covered in other chapters, mentors are under even more pressure. So, how can you promote positive pressure after observations with beginning teachers? It is beneficial for you to review the connection of these indicators to Student-Centered Mentoring (Figure 5.9). This will help you to promote the positive pressure following an observation experience.

KEEPING IT STUDENT CENTERED

It may be tempting to put off the debrief portion of an observation or postpone a follow-up conversation when things get busy. Instead, prioritize those things by instilling a sense of urgency to each observation component in order to support your mentee's desire to help students grow.

Figure 5.9 Student-Centered Connection to Positive Pressure Indicators

Promoting Positive Pressure With Student-Centered Mentoring	
Sense of focused urgency	• Focused on the needs and growth of students • Drivers of their own learning just like we hope for students
Partnership and peers	• Collective mindset around believing in all students • Collaborative reflection between mentees and mentors
Transparency of data	• Discussing student evidence and learning regularly • Openness about goals and problem-solving of next steps
Non-punitive accountability	• Showing vulnerability and having an innovator's learning mindset • Promoting peer-to-peer accountability
Irresistible synergy	• Move student and teacher learning forward through an alliance • Encouragement and celebration

Incorporated from Sweeney (2015)

Just as one mentor, Teena Pirkle, said, "The power of collaboration and helping each other remember strategies and practices that help our students more is so amazing!" Her mentee, Lindsay, who we heard from in Chapter 2, couldn't agree more with that. As you can see with their thinking, effective mentoring conversations are one way to lead new teachers to take further action in growing their craft. That is one of the key ways to use positive pressure to transfer practices into daily habits. Direct your attention to peer-to-peer accountability as you move into the next action step, focus on adding ways to hold each other accountable following observations.

MENTOR TIP

Joining up with your mentee in at least the planning stage of the observation process and promoting a positive observation experience will support the synergy of your mentoring partnership.

ACTION STEP #2: HELP EACH OTHER REMAIN ACCOUNTABLE

Peer-to-peer accountability is by now built nicely into your mentoring partnership. The important aspect of observational learning is accountability to follow through with the ideas afterward. Because of the inherent accountability already built into the mentoring partnership, it provides an increased chance of implementation. What do you, as a mentor, do to encourage actionable next steps to support that work?

▶ Conduct a follow-up after the observation(s)

▶ Set goals for implementation

▶ Check in on goal progress

▶ Take video of instructional practice

▶ Ask reflective questions of current students

Have a follow-up with your mentee after every observation. Whether it was a peer observation of you or a colleague or peer observation rounds that your mentee individually took part in, you will be empowered to hear your mentee's takeaways. If you were able to have a shared learning lab experience with your mentee, find a time afterwards to share your noticings from the experience as a duo. Over the years of observation experiences with new teachers, as well as mentors, I have noticed three areas in group attendees' takeaways: relationships, assessment, and reflection (Figure 5.10). Discuss your noticings within these three areas. The two of you may see your takeaways in the examples or you may have additional ideas. Through this process, you have an avenue to continue the conversation and build on your shared learning with further discussions as well.

Figure 5.10 Mentee/Mentor Observation Trends

Relationships	• Opportunity to strengthen partnership with mentee and vice versa
	• Ways to build classroom community
	• Ways to build relationships with students
Assessment	• Ways to be responsive to student needs
	• Informal assessment ideas during all parts of lessons/activities
	• Informal assessment that guides small groups formation
Reflection	• Reflect on student learning compared to their own students
	• Commonalities of what others share about instruction

Think back to the reflection on goals in Chapter 4. The last step in the process was to create an action plan for the remainder of the year, including at least one detail to attempt next week, next month, and by the end of the year. This action plan is the perfect place to embed the takeaways from the observational learning. If you completed the observation(s) prior to the collaborative session, refer to the observation takeaways when choosing ideas for next steps. An added benefit will be to revisit the mentee's goals and action plan regularly, revising along the way. It doesn't hurt to set new goals or shift the plan a different direction, depending on your mentee's needs and learning from observations.

KEEPING IT STUDENT CENTERED

There are times when a mentee will get sidetracked and focus mostly on the fact that they didn't know the specific content taught in an observation. Reiterate a balance with the content and the process of teaching students. Be sure to ask questions similar to, "How was it taught?" and "How do you know the students learned?"

Other ideas to promote accountability are reflective questioning and continuous discussion about the observation experiences. The main qualities of the reflective questions are open ended and student centered. You can use any moment to guide further conversations that bring the observation noticings back to the forefront of attention or make a note in a good place so you remember. Otherwise, both you and your mentee will easily forget the details. Incorporate these questions into your regular check-ins with your mentee:

- What did you notice about the students' response to instructional moves by the teacher?

- How are the students interacting and engaged in the lesson or activity?

- What did you notice about dialogue between students and teachers?

- How do students transition from one activity to another?

- What support might teachers be using to build student independence?

- How does the teacher coach/support all students?

- What level of rigor are students using during the lesson or activity?

- How can students be owners of their own learning?

One last opportunity to support implementation is to video your teaching or your work with students. It is important to set up the camera to focus on the whole room or the whole group of students when videoing instruction with a student-centered lens. Ideally, you want to pick an area that is connected to the observation experiences in order to visibly see the ideas you or your mentee are trying out. For example, if your goal is related to engagement, you could record students on the rug during a read aloud and pay close attention to their turn-and-talks. The fun in this part is to encourage each other to "spy" on your students' learning and then make time to look back on it, pause, and reflect. The reflection will promote amazing discussions around other ways to adjust teaching. Another way to promote the positive pressure and inspire each other is by watching the videos together. Above all, you will have the chance to notice the impact you have on your students, and this is a practice both you and your mentee should partake in. I encourage you to take the leap first and model the vulnerability for your mentee.

MENTOR TIP

Follow-up more than once with your mentee about how the two of you can incorporate techniques that you each learned from observations. This is where keeping those notes will prove to be helpful. Jot a reminder in your calendar to revisit the notes together and even commit to trying another idea from the takeaway list.

FROM THE LENS OF A NEW TEACHER

How Allison Found Instructional Clarity Through Varied Observations

In Chapter 4, we heard from Rodney and Natalie about their collaborative work. Now, we have the opportunity to hear about the continuous impact of mentoring from Natalie's mentee, Allison. She joined their first-grade team after having taught a year in a private school. Allison was very interested in taking in as much learning as she could through observations. She asked to observe other colleagues on her team and in the building, as well as participated in a mentor/mentee learning lab with Natalie. Here is Allison's perspective of the learning opportunities and benefits to her teaching:

As a new teacher, I am soaking in all kinds of new learning. Observing other teachers has been extremely beneficial to me because I have learned so many new ideas or ways to do things. When I observed Natalie, I loved how she had the kids engaged and they were using their whiteboards and other resources during the lesson. Now, I have been giving my students resources (like checklists, lists of strategies, blends and diagraphs charts) to have on hand when they are working, and I have seen so much growth and engagement when they have something to use, or in front of them.

I love observing lots of different teachers because every teacher does things differently. My college reading class was not great, so I feel like I needed the most support in teaching reading. Watching the reading interventionists amazed me! The reading interventionists have their lessons so well planned and consistent. Learning how to teach children to read can be very overwhelming, but the Reading Interventionist showed me that it doesn't have to be that challenging. One of the main takeaways I have had from the Reading Interventionists is a guided reading template to use when I am planning my small groups. It is so simple, but since I am new, I didn't even know where to start. The template really pinpoints the targets for what I should be teaching and when. They also gave me a list of characteristics for readers so that I have an idea of what skills each reader needs.

To top off those learning experiences, I was able to go to a learning lab with Natalie too. It stuck with me that there is not one right way to do anything. You need to constantly try new things until you find something that works for you and your students. I also realized from watching the other teachers that sometimes it looks so easy for them, but they might have tried 1000 different things before they found that strategy that worked for them. After the partner learning lab, Natalie and I both decided to make reading goal bookmarks for our students. We noticed the teacher using them and we thought that would be great for our students. Natalie made them for her class, as well as mine, and we started using them with our students right away. We had lots of conversations about how we were using them with students and how we could make them better. We even suggested the idea to the rest of our team.

Seeing multiple teachers gives me the opportunity to try a bunch of new ideas and then decide which one works best for me. I noticed all of the different ways teachers present new information to their students. The reason I love learning labs most is because I get so many new ideas and was able to collaborate with Natalie about what we saw way after the fact. It was also nice for both of us to try out some of the strategies and ideas we saw, then talk to each other about how they were working in our classrooms. After we tried something, we could then give each other tips on how to make it better, or how to make it work for our classrooms. The best part of all this is, if I try something I saw and it doesn't work out, I have so many more ideas from so many other great teachers to try with my kids.

The amazing result of observational learning is having the opportunity to hear about the impact. Allison was by far greatly impacted from the learning opportunities of seeing her colleagues interact with students in the area of reading, her focus. The clarity each moment provided Allison gave her specific next steps that she is still using in her classroom today. It did help to have her mentor, Natalie, follow up

(Continued)

(Continued)

through conversations and problem-solve with her on how to best adjust their practices. Most importantly, Allison loved having a partner in the work, Natalie, and sharing the new ideas with their team together. The power of the collaborative work has come full circle!

MENTOR TIP

Share this lens experience with your mentee and highlight Allison's perspective: Observing others and trying something with the understanding that if it doesn't work out, you have so many more ideas from so many other great teachers to try.

FROM THE LENS OF A MENTOR

How Casey and Her Mentee Supported Each Other With Learning Labs

Casey is a first-grade teacher at Wabash Elementary in Foristell, Missouri, west of St. Louis. She has always been a teacher who loves learning from videos and observations of other teachers. Her willingness to record herself is a strength as well. Casey's mentee, Jenna, was a first-year teacher and as willing to learn as her. They both had the opportunity to help open a new building. The two of them are a model of holding each other accountable in a true team style and continue to work together. Casey sums up her mentoring experience with some big takeaways:

Having another person to work with is incredibly beneficial— especially as a new teacher, but even more so as a mentor. My mentee and I were always able to bounce ideas off of each other and share things that we would see in training sessions, videos, and observations. It was always beneficial to do the work together because each of us picked up on different pieces throughout these experiences.

One particular memory is of us attending a learning lab together. The part that really stuck with me is the way the host teacher started her mini lessons for reading. She had such a great routine of reviewing sight words, blends and digraphs, and an alphabet chart. It was all student led and we both loved to see that! I implemented this strategy right away when we got back from our learning lab and we both continued to do so.

I also remember having many conversations about intentional planning of small groups before and after the learning lab experience. We were able to have a focus and see some amazing examples of planning out differentiated small groups, and then in turn have powerful conversations about our own students and how we can plan specific activities for them during small groups. It is always helpful to plan with someone else and get different ideas from them. To make it even better we were able to collaborate with teachers from other schools at the learning lab and gain insight into ways they run their small groups. The other bonus was we then carried on the conversation with our first-grade team members once we got back to our school and planned how we could fit some of the things we saw into our daily reading and writing workshop.

It was really helpful to have open conversations with my mentee about what we saw in our learning lab and how we could implement different ideas into our own classrooms. The same process was what guided our discussions when in training and in other observations. I have seen such great benefits from reviewing these important instructional elements each and every day. I am so glad to look back on this work with Jenna still today!

Casey continues to instill the importance of learning together with her teaching comrades. She is an example of a mentor who promotes the value of constantly refining her craft. Her mentoring partnership showcases the buildup of the Student-Centered Mentoring layers with the learning she took on and the collective mindset approach. Then, to extend the partnership with joint observational experiences, she helped set up her mentee for further success and impacted so many students with her mentoring approach.

 MENTOR TIP

Center your conversations similar to Casey's mentoring approach—keep in mind your mentee's focus and promote ways to visualize that in other classrooms together, while taking away new strategies for your own classroom as well.

RECAP AND REFLECT

Mentees and mentors discover the empowerment of learning and reflecting together through varied learning opportunities. All teachers find that observations provide a visual understanding that amazing learning opportunities can happen in classrooms next door, down the hall, or in a nearby school. So whether you get to join your mentee in the observation or follow-up in reflective conversations, learning through students opens up learning from each other. This third layer of support includes multiple observation options to make student learning applicable to new teachers and mentors. You can add on ways to hold each other accountable through actionable next steps by promoting follow-up to observations, goal setting, check-ins, and even videoing. You and your mentee's growth will then impact even more students.

MENTOR INQUIRY REFLECTION

Think back to your guiding questions at the beginning of the chapter. Take some time to reflect on the questions that follow as well as use the Rubric for Student-Centered Mentoring Section #5 to help set goals and make a plan for yourself (Figure 5.11).

1. How can you promote positive pressure in your mentoring partnership?

2. What instructional strategy focus can you help your mentee identify as they work to increase impact on students in their beginning years?

3. How can you embed student-centered observations into your work with your mentee?

4. Which Student-Centered Mentoring success criteria would you choose to support your mentoring partnership?

5. What are some initial action steps you and your mentee can take to gain teacher clarity?

Figure 5.11 Rubric for Student-Centered Mentoring

#5: Provide Shared Learning Opportunities		
Beginner	**Emerging**	**Innovative**
The mentor is understanding of the need to participate in observational learning and may pose for their mentee to do so solely.	The mentor is striving to learn from others in one or two ways and encourages their mentee to participate in a learning opportunity as well.	The mentor is learning alongside their mentee through varied opportunities, and both grow in their teacher clarity.

Success Criteria

- I can provide options of several observation types to grow my mentee's instructional repertoire.

- I can guide my mentee's observational look-fors to be focused on student-learning strategies.

- I can join my mentee in a mixture of observational experiences.

- I can set next steps in conjunction with my mentee following our observational learning.

- I can follow up with my mentee and collaborate around our learning.

6

PARTNER WITH A COACH OR COLLEAGUE IN A MENTOR COACHING CYCLE

Strategies for Utilizing Mentor Coaching Cycles

Strategy #1: Use Student-Centered Coaching When Collaborating With a Third Person

Action Step #1: Work With an Instructional Coach or Another Colleague

Action Step #2: Set the Foundation With a Student-Centered Coaching Structure

Strategy #2: Organize a Mentor Coaching Cycle With Your Mentee

Action Step #1: Introduce Mentor Coaching Cycles to Your Mentee

Action Step #2: Decide on a Mentor Coaching Cycle Structure and Norms

Action Step #3 Determine a Mentor Coaching Cycle Goal and Targets That Meet Everyone's Needs

Strategy #3: Analyze the Impact on Student Achievement

Action Step #1: Make the Connection to Collective Teacher Efficacy

Action Step #2: Celebrate the Mentor Coaching Cycle Success

When I think about what effective Mentor Coaching Cycles look like, I can't help but think of my personal experience with sushi. I look back on how I grew to love the food and consider how it felt much like being a brand-new teacher. My husband, Jay, and I first had the opportunity to try sushi when we were eating dinner with another couple. They were accustomed to having sushi regularly and recommended we try it. Both of us were watching cautiously as our friends took the chopsticks between their fingers like it was something they do all of the time. I was very hesitant to even attempt to eat it, let alone use new utensils. However, since we had someone with experience guiding us on what to try, we were much more likely to go outside our comfort zone than if we had tried to navigate the sushi menu on our own. To my surprise, we both liked it and continue to eat it, even seeking out the best places to have it.

Fast-forward a few years. Jay was encouraging me to try wasabi with my sushi, but I was always against it because I associated wasabi with hot sauce, which I do not like. Plus, I felt like I had already taken a big step by eating sushi in the first place, so why rock the boat? Eventually I agreed to try it, and his guidance and persuasion helped me to add another way to enjoy eating sushi.

Jay's encouragement, willingness, and support were like the characteristics of a mentor, and the couple was like our instructional coach. The progression of my sushi experience is similar to a Mentor Coaching Cycle process—not only is the new teacher learning but so is the mentor. The addition of wasabi to my sushi "repertoire" showcases how the long-term effects from the original coaching experience can continue with new teachers and mentors. Not every teacher is going to be able to pick up all skills during the Mentor Coaching Cycle, but having the mentor as a part of the collective group allows strategies and instructional practices to be added when the new teacher is ready. Mentor Coaching Cycles can provide that support as you both continue to build collective teacher efficacy—and in turn, double the impact of student achievement.

This steers us into the last section of the Student-Centered Mentor layers: in-depth support (Figure 6.1). This layer is where the action of trying out instructional practices embeds habits and efficacious beliefs for mentees and mentors alongside another colleague.

Figure 6.1 Layers of Student-Centered Mentoring With Key Ideas

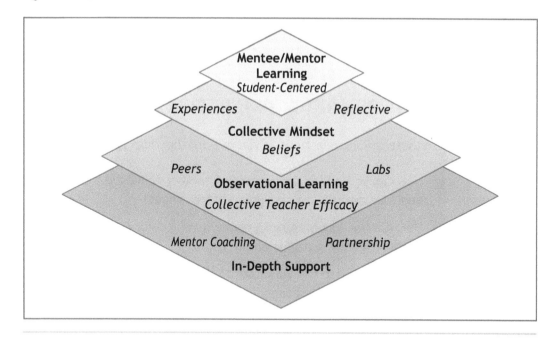

Mentee/Mentor
Learning
Student-Centered

Experiences   *Reflective*

Collective Mindset
Beliefs

Peers   *Labs*

Observational Learning
Collective Teacher Efficacy

Mentor Coaching   *Partnership*

In-Depth Support

WHAT IS THIS CHAPTER ABOUT?

In this chapter, you will learn strategies to

➤ Use Student-Centered Coaching options when collaborating with a third person

➤ Go in-depth with organizing Mentor Coaching Cycles

➤ Promote furthering the impact on student achievement

Within this chapter, I will describe a structure for you and your mentee to learn together alongside a third person in Mentor Coaching Cycles using a student-centered approach. It is optimal if the third person is an instructional coach. However, if an instructional coach is not a resource in your building, consider adding another colleague, such as a teacher leader on the staff or even an administrator. As I describe the process for Mentor Coaching Cycles, tips for including another colleague will be given throughout. To prepare for the work, it is helpful to understand that instructional coaching provides teachers with in-the-moment learning centered on increasing the potential of effective instructional practices. Teachers who have experienced coaching have commonly done so individually. Mentor Coaching Cycles differ in that the instructional coaching cycles include both the mentee and mentor with the focus on the students from both classrooms. From there, you can increase the impact for both your class as well as your mentee.

MENTOR INQUIRY PRE-REFLECTION

Use these guiding questions as you explore the ideas in this chapter.

1. How can you utilize the support of another colleague to help you and your mentee increase your student impact?

2. How can you incorporate components of Mentor Coaching Cycles in your mentoring partnership?

3. What connection can you make to the states of collective teacher efficacy that can be connected to student achievement growth?

WHAT ARE MENTOR COACHING CYCLES?

To understand Mentor Coaching Cycles, I will first review why they were created: in-depth support and consistency. I began my first year as a literacy coach in multiple elementary buildings in the fastest-growing district in the state of Missouri. That meant we had a large number of new teachers, and in turn, principals wanted us to begin our instructional coaching cycles with those teachers. It also meant I had to say "no" to coaching more seasoned teachers because I was unable to fit them into my schedule, which did not feel right. One afternoon, I walked out of a new teacher's classroom and ran into her mentor, who asked, "What can I do to continue helping her in the work you all are trying once your cycle is over?" The answer was not easy. We ended up having several conversations that raised even more questions about how to best assist this phenomenal beginning teacher as well as how I could support her mentor through my coaching work.

The next steps consisted of a lot of trial-and-error. In the end, the Mentor Coaching Cycle was born, and I had the added benefit of widening the net of my coaching support to include both new teachers and their mentors. With a complex endeavor such as teaching, it is extremely difficult to reach and then maintain high levels of performance and student achievement without help; the most effective help commonly comes in the form of instructional coaching (Marzano & Simms, 2013). The joint collaboration of another colleague or coach, along with you, the mentor, is another layer of support for a beginning teacher. Joyce and Showers (as cited in Marzano & Simms, 2013) found that "a large and dramatic increase in transfer of training—effect size of 1.42—occurs when coaching is added to an initial training experience" (as cited in Marzano & Simms, 2013, p. 5). What better way to promote that transfer of a mentee's newly learned practices than to add the layer of instructional coaching to the mentoring partnership!

As was mentioned in earlier chapters, teachers are also under enormous pressure to help students effectively. Schools should encourage a network of peer support that encourages this positive pressure of continued improvement (Foltos, 2013; Sweeney, 2015). The same indicators we talked about in Chapter 5—a sense of focused urgency, partnership and peers, transparency of data, non-punitive accountability, and irresistible synergy (as cited in Sweeney, 2015)—can help the triad have effective conversations and promote peer-to-peer accountability so that student and teacher learning can move forward. Additionally, the limited experience of teachers, an overabundance of data, and lack of systems to analyze student results can be significantly reduced through coaching conversations (Sweeney, 2011). So why not utilize this type of support to help coach your mentee?

A Mentor Coaching Cycle is when you and your mentee participate together in an instructional coaching cycle. As you and your mentee plan alongside instructional coaches, everyone can share ideas with each other. The instructional coach (or qualified colleague) can then co-teach in both classrooms to modeled effective instructional techniques for new teachers. Mentor Coaching Cycles showed growth in both mentor and mentees making small changes in instructional practices, which in turn made considerable impacts on student learning. When collaborating about the co-teaching, both mentors and mentees are able to see what works in improving student outcomes as they share strategies, methods, activities, and samples of student work (Tschannen-Moran & Barr, 2004). The group atmosphere promotes consistency of information with beginning teachers as well. Do not worry if an instructional coach is not in your building. As you read further, you will learn ways to include another colleague to work with you both.

WHY SHOULD YOU CONSIDER A MENTOR COACHING CYCLE?

Let's think back to Natalie in an earlier chapter. As a beginning teacher, she was the true definition of a sponge for knowledge. Her mentor, Rodney, was extremely supportive and helped her students grow because of their partnership. They participated in peer observations along with a Mentor Coaching Cycle and found both to be impactful with their students. Now, Natalie is a mentor herself. She has come full circle, as she learned to use the same collaborative techniques and instructional practices with her mentee through a Mentor Coaching Cycle as well. One of her mentee's, Allison, needs was supporting the student-teacher relationship piece. As with Natalie's mentee experience, we knew the benefit of both observing other teachers in the building as well as utilizing a Mentor Coaching Cycle, and Allison was on board. Naturally, we made the connection to building a positive classroom environment as a team, and both of their classrooms of students profited from the work.

This directly supports the powerful benefits of developing a mentor and mentee's collective efficacy through a Mentor Coaching Cycle. It was just as a fellow researcher stated, "Because of this self and group sense of efficacy, I argue that teachers developed a strong sense of loyalty and commitment to the coach and to literacy coaching" (Ferguson, 2014, p. 27). Natalie yearned for the same structure and guidance with Allison. Not only did Natalie seek out a Mentor Coaching Cycle for her and Allison, but Natalie also made several connections back to her new teacher experience with the Mentor Coaching Cycle.

What happens when a coach leaves a cycle with any teacher? The hope is that strategies and practices continue for the teacher within the classroom. But add in being a new teacher and trying to survive the beginning years. Therefore, you provide the sustainability of practices and can help deepen your mentee's professional development long after the cycle is over. Keep in mind that coaching is more about asking the right questions than telling people what to do and should be about helping teachers maintain their best performance on their own (Marzano & Simms, 2013). Communication and collaboration skills are highly important for effective coaching as well as mentoring. Take into consideration what you can use in your mentoring partnership following the mentor coaching experience.

STRATEGIES FOR UTILIZING MENTOR COACHING CYCLES

As you read through these strategies, you will find that communication is key in preparation for Mentor Coaching Cycles. These strategies cover the details that will make your preparation easier and clearer. I will also share Student-Centered Coaching techniques within this chapter as well. Each strategy has multiple action steps to walk you through the process. Read through each strategy and then form a plan of action so that you and your mentee can reap the benefits from a Mentor Coaching Cycle.

STRATEGY #1: USE STUDENT-CENTERED COACHING WHEN COLLABORATING WITH A THIRD PERSON

This strategy is particularly beneficial as you ask a coach or colleague to join you in providing your mentee with the in-depth support of a Mentor Coaching Cycle. It is key to set the foundation built on the Student-Centered Coaching model, which Sweeney and Harris describe in depth in *The Essential Guide For Student-Centered Coaching* (Sweeney & Harris, 2020. Since I began coaching, I have used the Student-Centered Coaching model and have found it to be a successful instructional coaching approach with not only regular cycles but also with beginning teachers and mentors. Going hand-in-hand with Student-Centered Mentoring, Student-Centered Coaching can help with the pressures mentors and mentees face: "By focusing the lens on students, we can diffuse the existing pressures we feel related to 'resistant' teachers since the focus is not on improving them, but instead is on improving the achievement of their students" (Sweeney, 2011, p. 15).

ACTION STEP #1: WORK WITH AN INSTRUCTIONAL COACH OR ANOTHER COLLEAGUE

As a mentor, it is usually not feasible to spend a large chunk of time in your mentee's classroom co-teaching to help build their use of effective instructional practices. This is where including your instructional coach in a joint coaching cycle will provide you and your mentee with the opportunity to co-teach. If an instructional coach is unavailable, consider another colleague who may have the opportunity to step into that role for about three to four hours per week. At the start of this collaboration, it is important to have a discussion about norms and roles for each person in the coaching experience. See Figure 6.2 for an overview of the specific roles each person takes with a Mentor Coaching Cycle. You will note that there are multiple options depending on if you have an instructional coach or another colleague join your mentoring partnership in this experience.

Figure 6.2 **Mentor Coaching Cycle Roles to Consider in Conjunction With a Coach or Colleague**

Mentor Coaching Cycle With an Instructional Coach	Mentor Coaching Cycle With Another Colleague
• Coach takes the lead in setting the stage for the coaching cycle work • Coach co-teaches with both the mentor and mentee • Coach uses strengths-based feedback	• Mentor and colleague discuss who takes the lead, possibly sharing the role as needed • Mentor and colleague co-teach with the mentee • Mentor and colleague use strengths-based feedback
• Mentor participates in planning sessions weekly • Mentor uses strengths-based feedback • Mentor continues to provide support for mentee when coaching cycle is complete	• Mentor and colleague participate in weekly planning sessions • Mentor continues to provide support for mentee when coaching cycle is complete

One option to make particular note of is that you and a colleague could alternate between coaching the mentee. More so than anything, the discussion of who is going to take the lead is imperative. It does not have to be you, the mentor. Your colleague could take the lead as a facilitator of the experience. It is important to discuss the structure of the Mentor Coaching Cycle with the instructional coach or colleague before including the mentee. Then, decide together the options for co-teaching and co-planning. Flexibility is key, and each week the work together could look different. So revisit and adjust roles as well as norms a few times throughout the cycle work.

MENTOR TIP

It is extremely valuable to discuss the norms and roles with the instructional coach or colleague before starting the Mentor Coaching Cycle work. When everyone is clear on that, it makes the process much more beneficial for mentees. Before starting the Mentor Coaching Cycle, also discuss how the process will look with the mentee in order to keep from overwhelming them during the cycle.

ACTION STEP #2: SET THE FOUNDATION WITH A STUDENT-CENTERED COACHING STRUCTURE

The focus of Mentor Coaching Cycles is to promote a student-centered approach with both new teachers and mentors. Sweeney & Harris (2020) outline a student-centered approach to instructional coaching and follows an approximate four- to six-week cycle through the process of six stages. As I have found with practicing Student-Centered Coaching, keeping students at the forefront of all coaching conversations allows for growth to occur with both students and teachers. Teachers feel supported in improving their instructional practices when they participate in instructional coaching cycles. So what are these four- to six-week coaching cycles? A general definition is that Student-Centered Coaching cycles are four- to six-week rotations in classrooms and planning where the focus is on the use of student evidence (Sweeney & Harris, 2020). The teacher and instructional coach work together through an assess-plan-teach format.

MENTOR TIP

Team coaching can help new teachers and mentors incorporate all of the elements of effective professional development.
Start thinking about how you can align the instructional coaching support with the learning your mentee receives in their induction sessions and other professional learning. A perfect example could be a Mentor Coaching Cycle during Reading Workshop, if your mentee has been focused on learning in the area of reading.

Think back to Chapter 1's comparison of coaching in a teacher-centered and student-centered approach. The focus of typical coaching is on the teacher rather than the primary attention being on students. Student-Centered Coaching is an instructional coaching design that consists of these key characteristics (Sweeney & Harris, 2020):

- Four to six weeks for a coaching cycle duration

- Planning one time per week

- Co-teaching in classrooms two to three times per week

- Goals and targets are set at initial meetings

Coaching with new teachers should utilize these Student-Centered Coaching model characteristics as the basis for the work. If the instructional coach or colleague you work with is not familiar with the above characteristics, encourage them to look into the model in Sweeney and Harris's (2020) *The Essential Guide for Student-Centered Coaching*. Their website is also continuously updated with resources and information. As you think of this option, keep in mind there is an intense focus on using student data to set a coaching cycle goal. Student data then drives all instructional decisions. In the next strategy, I will describe other aspects of the model as they connect more to Mentor Coaching Cycles.

KEEPING IT STUDENT CENTERED

It may come up that both you and the instructional coach want to answer your mentee's resource questions during co-planning. Just remember, the more centered around students' learning the coaching work is, the greater the impact will be on student learning (Sweeney, 2011). I recommend answering resource questions outside of the co-planning time in order to maximize time with the instructional coach.

STRATEGY #2: ORGANIZE A MENTOR COACHING CYCLE WITH YOUR MENTEE

Let's take the Student-Centered Coaching structure and blend it with Mentor Coaching Cycles. Think of it as you and the new teacher working together in a two-person cycle with an instructional coach using the Student-Centered Coaching model. You will want to be transparent with your mentee on the set-up and communicate the process of setting a standards-based goal and targets. Being clear from the start will set your partnership up for an amazing experience of co-planning and co-teaching. Students' achievement is then impacted as a result of the trio's improved practices.

ACTION STEP #1: INTRODUCE MENTOR COACHING CYCLES TO YOUR MENTEE

As a mentor, you will want to discuss how Mentor Coaching Cycles work with the instructional coach or colleague you invite into the collaborative partnership. These key attributes are recommended when implementing Mentor Coaching Cycles:

- Classroom instructional time is shared in varied ways between the new teacher and mentor.

- The mentee and mentor choose goals, targets, and coaching moves.

- There is balance in coaching both the mentee and mentor with strengths-based feedback.

- Protocols and varied ways to learn from each other are incorporated to allow for the sustainability of next steps.

- Conversations are centered on student evidence, and the evidence is used to drive next steps.

- Flexibility is the key to success!

Share these attributes as you introduce Mentor Coaching Cycles to your mentee. It is also important for you to explain the importance of your participation in a Mentor Coaching Cycle. As with the sushi scenario, you, their mentor, can give further support as time passes through follow-up planning. Through a Mentor Coaching Cycle, you can now be armed with the knowledge and ability to help sustain the continued work of your mentee. Essentially, a mentor is a coach to the mentee as well, therefore the "working alongside of the new teacher" mindset can live on in your partnership. Just like the follow-up to observations, follow-up with Mentor Coaching Cycles is important for continued growth of your mentee. Remember to bring up regularly how the two of you can incorporate techniques that you each learned from the cycle work. Keep those notes during the cycle planning sessions and make a reminder in your calendar.

MENTOR TIP

In a Mentor Coaching Cycle, the coach can serve as a model for you too. Pay close attention to the types of questions asked and coaching language that will add value to your mentoring role.

ACTION STEP #2: DECIDE ON A MENTOR COACHING CYCLE STRUCTURE AND NORMS

The classroom instruction time in a Mentor Coaching Cycle should be varied between the beginning teacher and you, the mentor. It is easy to assume that more of the instructional coach's time should be spent in a mentee's classroom, but in reality, the time co-teaching in each person's classroom is dependent on the partnership's goals and targets as well as which week it is in the cycle. Co-teaching within a week should be flexible from one week to the next. The three to four hours per week that another colleague needs to commit to the Mentor Coaching Cycle includes a co-planning session and the two to three classroom instruction sessions (balanced between both you and your mentee). The time is approximate because the length of the co-planning session and classroom instruction sessions can vary. Figure 6.3 is a comparison of the structure of an individual instructional coaching cycle and a Mentor Coaching Cycle.

Figure 6.3 **Structure Comparison for Individual Versus Mentor Coaching Cycles**

Individual Instructional Coaching Cycle Example	Mentor Coaching Cycle Examples
• Two to three days per week co-teaching for entire class period • Planning one time per week	• Two days mentee/one day mentor • Three days mentee/one day mentor • Split some weeks evenly • Half of one class period in one room and then switch

If another teacher colleague is taking the role of the instructional coach, you can still use the Student-Centered Coaching Cycle structure. The only adjustment would be that the colleague and you, the mentor, take on a joint role of coach/mentor. Typically, an instructional coach would spend time going in and out of both the new teacher and mentor's classrooms; however, in a Mentor Coaching Cycle, the mentor and colleague can work out how to co-teach with the mentee. One way to do this would be to cover each other's classroom during a plan time or break to allow co-teaching to take place. It is also possible for the mentor and colleague to co-teach together. The beauty of this option is the flexibility.

An initial meeting between you and the instructional coach will need to include conversations about the shared responsibility of supporting your mentee and how co-teaching takes place in the classroom. Then, you can invite the mentee to participate in an initial discussion and review the possibilities of the co-teaching options. Co-teaching options could include using voiceovers, demonstration, freeze-frame, mirror, whispering in, notice and name, teaching in tandem, and so forth. Talk specifically about how to interact together during class time. You will also want to ask who is going to do what when co-planning weekly. Discussing these topics could follow a progression of questions:

- How will we co-teach together?
- Who will teach what part of a lesson/activity?
- What will the other teacher do when not teaching?
- What are some ways we can gather student evidence?
- How will we share our notes about students?

MENTOR TIP

For a great resource on co-teaching strategies to use in a Mentor Coaching Cycle, read *Student-Centered Coaching: The Moves* by Sweeney and Harris. This text has note-taking tools to collect student evidence to go along with the moves.

The other component of setting up Mentor Coaching Cycles is having norms for planning conversations. I recommend utilizing the Seven Norms of Collaboration from *The Adaptive School* (Garmston & Wellman, 2016) to balance conversations between you, your mentee, and the instructional coach.

1. Pausing
2. Paraphrasing
3. Posing Questions
4. Putting Ideas on the Table
5. Providing Data
6. Paying Attention to Self and Others
7. Presuming Positive Intentions

The use of questioning and limiting responses as a coach and mentor are key to help promote thoughts from the mentee.

ACTION STEP #3: DETERMINE A MENTOR COACHING CYCLE GOAL AND TARGETS THAT MEET EVERYONE'S NEEDS

As we dive a little deeper into Mentor Coaching Cycle work, it is important to have joint goals. This is something you should include in an initial meeting and will repeatedly revisit in planning conversations. Teasing out the potential goal depends on the current unit or standards you and your mentee are working on with their groups of students. That is why the Mentor Coaching Cycle works best for a mentor and mentee who are teaching the same grade level or content courses. It could also be that you are working on a similar instructional skill that can work across content. It is helpful for the instructional coach to take on the role of asking these initial questions. Great initial questions for the instructional coach to ask each of you are, "What would you like your students to accomplish?" and "How is that connected to standards?" Once the initial thoughts are noted, additional questioning can be used to uncover the joint goal focus on student learning. Figure 6.4 is an example of a Mentor Coaching Cycle goal with targets.

Figure 6.4 Mentor Coaching Cycle Goal/Target Example (4th grade)

Student-Centered Goal
• Students will be able to infer the change of character traits in connection to themes and explain with text evidence.

Learning Targets
• I can self-assess using the learning progressions.
• I can set appropriate goals for reading.
• I can communicate about my reading life to others.
• I can explain character traits using exact word choices.
• I can develop word skills.
• I can explain the theme of a text.
• I can select the appropriate evidence to support my thinking.

The differentiation for the mentee and yourself is important, just like it is for students. Learning targets are one of the ways to value needs from both sets of students. Since learning targets are pathways to achieving a goal, it could also be that your mentee may need a different target than you. Even if you and your mentee have different needs, you may find that the majority of the targets will be necessary for both of your classrooms.

Take the goal from Figure 6.4 as an example. Tori, the beginning teacher, and Diane, the mentor, wanted to work around the goal that included understanding of character traits and themes. We chose our targets to get to the goal by including a mixture of skills and reading habits. One of the targets, "I can develop word skills," was an additional target that Diane and I co-taught together. Tori and I were unable to get to that work, as the other targets were our priority based on her students' needs.

Remember the targets are meant to meet your students' needs as well as your mentee's students' needs. You need to model the practice of reflecting on student evidence and the impact of your teaching by including your student evidence in the mix as well. A general guideline for the number of targets for one individual is four to six. So if you have to add one or two targets to meet each set of needs, that is OK.

IN THE CLASSROOM

The learning targets are to be used with students. They can be set as the success criteria for self-assessing or to measure if students are meeting the Mentor Coaching Cycle goal in connection with the pre-assessment and post-assessment for the cycle. A target should be used when co-teaching and collecting student evidence in order to see the students who are making growth. Communicating a target with students is a best practice in any classroom.

STRATEGY #3: ANALYZE THE IMPACT ON STUDENT ACHIEVEMENT

Ultimately, the goal of any Mentor Coaching Cycle is improved instruction in order to increase student growth. Noted researcher Ferguson (2014) looked at how teachers, coaches, and principals viewed the success of literacy coaching in their schools, and she found that, "Teachers believed their teaching was better than before and that they were more effective because they saw success with students" (p. 27). A key part Ferguson (2014) noted was that, "Teachers felt that they were a team, working together to better student achievement" (p. 27). You, the mentor, can compound the success when working alongside a beginning teacher. Not only does instruction improve and student outcomes get reached at the same time, but also the coaching impact is doubled with Mentor Coaching Cycles. Coaching is specifically working toward student outcomes (Hattie, 2012). This strategy showcases how you can share that impact and increase collective teacher efficacy by doing so.

ACTION STEP #1: MAKE THE CONNECTION TO COLLECTIVE TEACHER EFFICACY

As a follow-up to your Mentor Coaching Cycle work, you should make the connection to the sources of collective teacher efficacy in understanding how to promote the cycle work further and increase collectiveness in your school. Thinking about coaching as "teamwork" can bypass many issues by diffusing much of the fear around change, allow teachers to think creatively about shared work, and can be an effective way to promote collaboration between teacher teams (Miller & Stewart, 2013). Collaboration is at the heart of collective teacher efficacy and shows up heavily in Mentor Coaching Cycles.

One particular Mentor Coaching Cycle that showcases a perfect example of the value of the collective efficacy was with Lindsay and her mentor Teena, both first-grade teachers. As we had our first meeting, Teena was honest with me and said she had never signed up for a cycle before with any coach. After discussing her hopes for student learning and the work of their upcoming reading unit, we chose to have our student goal about using reading strategies independently. It was the primary focus of this first-grade unit for building good reading habits, and Lindsay was hoping to get a great deal of guidance on how to grow her students as readers.

Teena had taught the unit in the previous year. With the help of her experience, we discussed how stamina and volume were important concepts in the unit and then decided a learning target needed to be, "I can be engaged in my reading." Our work around the engagement target also boosted both teachers' engagement. Lindsay really enjoyed creating shared booklets with students using interactive writing at instructional levels of texts. That spread to Teena and I co-teaching some of her groups in the same way. At the end of their Mentor Coaching Cycle, we reflected on our collaborative work. Lindsay shared how inspiring each other to try some new things gave them the courage to follow through. Teena (personal communication, August 29, 2017) added on at one point, "How can we go ahead and sign up for a cycle next year?" You and your mentee both develop the confidence and inspiration to learn more as a result of a Mentor Coaching Cycle. That efficacy can then easily spread to others in your school.

IN THE CLASSROOM

Teena loves sharing how much change occurred in her students' love of reading after a focus on the engagement target. One student in particular hated reading at the beginning of the year. Through our co-teaching and incorporating interactive writing with instructional level texts, he came to be a self-starter and enjoyed being a reader. Teena's account of him approaching her one morning saying, "I love, love, love reading!" brought us ALL to tears. Think about ways to embed a target or strategy to promote students to be independent in their own learning as well.

As we continue to reflect on the connection Mentor Coaching Cycles have on increasing collective teacher efficacy as the most in-depth approach to being student centered, let's revisit the figure from previous chapters. An additional column has been added to showcase the sources of collective teacher efficacy in relation to Mentor Coaching Cycles (Figure 6.5). What seems to be most impactful is mastery experiences. The moments with Teena and Lindsay are also examples of other sources, such as the social persuasion. Teena and Lindsay's cycle include several specifics, such as these:

➤ Their common goal based off of their hopes for students

➤ Targets that helped us have small successes along the way

➤ Increased confidence in their ability to help students grow as readers

➤ Their joint partnership in the Mentor Coaching Cycle that provided accountability with each other

Figure 6.5 Collective Teacher Efficacy Connection to Mentor Coaching Cycles

Sources of Efficacy	Definition	Layers of Support	Connection Explanation	Mentor Coaching Cycle Examples
Mastery Experiences	Trying something as a team and seeing success because of their actions	Mentor Coaching Cycles	Learning and growing together; achieving success resulting in increased confidence as a team	• Co-teaching • Weekly collaborative planning sessions • Reflective final meeting
Vicarious Experiences	Seeing others trying something and seeing success; making the connection they too can overcome challenges	New teacher and mentor training, labs and observations, Mentor Coaching Cycles	Planning lessons and observing colleagues; group inquiry and collaboration; case study of students	• Co-teaching • Planning next steps following pre-assessment • Discussing and sorting student evidence
Social Persuasion	Credible and trustworthy colleague persuades a team to try something new and overcome obstacles	New teacher and mentor training, Mentor Coaching Cycles	Student-Centered Training; learning with colleagues in similar roles; triad collaboration with coach	• Weekly collaborative planning sessions • Discussing what worked and didn't work in lessons
Affective States	Feeling successful when overcoming difficulty or anxiety about potential	Mentor Coaching Cycles	Collaborative reflection; problem-solving next steps; celebration of student growth	• Thinking aloud during co-teaching • Reflective meeting • Comparing pre- and post-assessment proficiency

> ## KEEPING IT STUDENT CENTERED
>
> It is natural to want to highlight your mentee's improved instruction first as you reflect. However, direct your attention to student evidence first in your planning conversations. Identifying student growth enhances the teacher's interest in the focus area of the Mentor Coaching Cycle, which makes a difference in their willingness to continue risk-taking. Consider thinking similarly to Teena and Lindsay, for example—both continue to seek out coaching cycles because of the power they see in how it helps students learn.

A common benefit that has been noted is how the triad collaboration helps build the group's beliefs about making a difference in all students' learning. When participants in Mentor Coaching Cycles are surveyed around some of these beliefs, it is most important to note the greatest increase in both the mentee and mentor perception of their impact on student learning. The belief statement, *"Learning takes place in my classroom because students are not worried about external factors of their home life,"* was the most noticeable. Teachers rated their beliefs from 1—strongly disagree—to 8—strongly agree. On average, beliefs increased for both mentees and mentors about 1 level or more from the start of the Mentor Coaching Cycle to the end (Brueggeman, 2018). Revisit your belief ratings with your mentee to see if you both had a similar increase.

ACTION STEP #2: CELEBRATE THE MENTOR COACHING CYCLE SUCCESS

At the end of the Mentor Coaching Cycle is a final reflection meeting. This is where the celebration of student impact takes place. Kelli and Amanda are another mentor partnership team I have worked with. In their Mentor Coaching Cycle reflection, Kelli (personal communication, October 17, 2017) noted that "Students were depending on their peers more rather than always coming to me." The pair realized Kelli's students could not have learned how to do that without getting the know-how from their co-planning. The collaboration encouraged positive pressure, as other Mentor Coaching Cycles discovered as well.

Mentors and mentees like the accountability and the push to get out of a learning pit. Through the partnership, they were able to uncover the student needs to help each other grow in their understanding as well. The conclusion is evident that new teachers need explicit support through mentors and coaches to help build their success to impact student learning. Celebrate the growth in student achievement for double the amount of students to promote collective efficacy across your building too.

KEEPING IT STUDENT CENTERED

Thinking back to earlier chapters, the value in celebrating our success with students is helpful in developing efficacious beliefs and confidence, especially for your mentee. Brainstorm ideas with your mentee about ways to celebrate the impact on students from your Mentor Coaching Cycle.

Taking the time to discuss the Mentor Coaching Cycle results leads you and your mentee to evaluate your impact on student learning. The analysis of student evidence then comes to be second nature for teachers because of modeling the process at the end of the cycle. After having the co-teaching and co-planning opportunities, teachers are able to observe student needs more easily and make adjustments on the spot. You and your mentee can continue to support each other after the Mentor Coaching Cycle and help each other see trends in a quicker manner. By continuing to collaborate, you are continuing to evaluate your impact on student learning in an effective way.

MENTOR TIP

Find a way to share the student results and takeaways from the Mentor Coaching Cycle with other colleagues. Maybe even ask your administrator for a moment in a staff meeting to share the student benefits!

FROM THE LENS OF A NEW TEACHER

How Jaden Was Empowered Through Student Evidence in a Mentor Coaching Cycle

Jaden was a second-year teacher in her education career, and she was moved from first grade to third grade as a result of decrease enrollment in first grade. So although she was a second-year teacher, she felt like it was her first all over again. That year brought many changes for not only Jaden but the entire third-grade team. Jaden was replacing a seasoned teacher who was moving onto a different role. Two of her teammates were only in their second year on the third-grade team, with only one of them having more than two years of experience. To add even more onto all of that, her mentor had only been in the grade level a year after returning from a yearlong leave of absence.

Jaden knew from her participation in a Mentor Coaching Cycle in her first year teaching that it was a powerful experience. Her mentor had not yet taken part in a coaching cycle but was eager to do so. I got the pleasure of acting as the instructional coach in their Mentor Coaching Cycle, and we found the results from the cycle to be exciting. Additionally, their students grew immensely in their achievement within the writing cycle, growing in proficiency from a 43% to 81% for Jaden's pre- to post-assessment of the cycle. Jaden's account of a moment in the cycle was centered around our evaluation of the impact on students' learning in writing.

> An aspect of our coaching cycle work that I really enjoyed and found most useful was conferencing with students about their learning. Dr. Brueggeman and I went around my classroom and had one-on-one conferences with the majority of my students at their desks about their opinion writing pieces. She asked them two questions, "what are you working on as a writer today?" and "what is the writing learning target today?" We were able to document student responses and their behaviors during independent writing time.

(Continued)

(Continued)

Afterwards, we shared the information with each other, and the students' responses were eye opening to me! I was able to get an idea of how many of my students grasped the learning target that day and those who were trying a specific target strategy in their own writing. I also found out which students were lost and needed guidance.

Dr. Brueggeman and my mentor did the same kind of work together. From that student evidence, my mentor and I were then able to compare observation notes, teaching styles, and strategies of what worked really well for her class and what I wanted to try in my own classroom. I thought this was a great way to learn from one another in our Mentor Coaching Cycle!

The power of our collaborative work together was focused on a writing goal. The goal was, "Students will be able to form an opinion and support it with key reasons." We were excited that students were able to communicate their successes and needs for achieving this goal. When we reflected on our cycle work, one of the instructional moves teachers picked up on were the modeling with examples. In addition, teachers realized the importance of showcasing how to help students in their personal assessment of whether they achieved the learning target for the day. Jaden had noted how this seemed like a small idea, but it was more impactful than she could have imagined.

MENTOR TIP

Share this Lens of a Mentee experience with your mentee and highlight Jaden's take on assessment: Move students along by getting them involved in assessing their own learning.

FROM THE LENS OF A MENTOR

How Teena Connected Accountability to the Aspect of Social Persuasion

I am excited to share a more detailed story from Lindsay's mentor, Teena. Teena was a reading interventionist before moving to a first-grade classroom. She and Lindsay were a perfect match, as Lindsay was most worried about teaching reading to her first graders after being a fifth-grade teacher in another state. We heard bits and pieces from the duo throughout Chapter 6, but here is Teena's reflection of the cycle where she makes a strong connection to social persuasion of collective teacher efficacy:

> We loved how the Mentor Coaching Cycle work helped us dissect data, recognize a need, and further research a strategy to then give it a try. A good teacher should always want to grow and meet the needs of students. A good coach can help with the process. It is exactly what every teacher truly needs. Getting to do that work with a partner teacher helps! Also, at the forefront of my mind has always been to realize I can learn just as much from my mentee. Lindsay's ability to pull out thinking from a curricular viewpoint was what was helpful to me.
>
> Many of our students had low self-efficacy when it came to reading. They centered their belief of themselves on the statement, "I can't read." Our goal was to help our students see themselves as readers, which would help them be successful in life. Specifically in the partner cycle, we tried an idea called massive practice. It was meant to help students have more access to books with support and up their volume of reading. We did a great deal of thinking aloud through our co-teaching and it was extremely helpful to share how we tried this in our classrooms. It was clear to us to move forward and share the idea with our team. They all bought into it as well, helping even more students.
>
> Success is overcoming fears and then seeing how something worked. Accountability is the successful benefit of a cycle. The triad of work in the Mentor Coaching Cycle set Lindsay and me up to talk daily, even after the cycle was over. Golden nuggets came from those conversations. Highlights were often shared from our work and how to deliver the golden nuggets. A shared load is a lighter load so all of us can have those golden nuggets. Going into the work with a mentee with the thought of what am I going to learn helps to uncover those golden nuggets even faster.

The after effects are still noted from this cycle work. In a follow-up meeting, Teena shared how she gained as much growth as her mentee noted when discussing the cycle work. Teena was so excited to share how she is still incorporating the cycle work in her classroom. Walking away from that follow-up meeting, we both felt that instructional practices were still being used, and even more students were continuing to benefit from our Mentor Coaching Cycle work. I can only imagine the impact on more students the two will continue to have from year to year.

(Continued)

(Continued)

MENTOR TIP

Consider Teena's takeaways of her Mentor Coaching Cycle—her willingness to want to help both sets of students and hold each other accountable as well.

RECAP AND REFLECT

Mentor Coaching Cycles are the in-depth layer of support that can be provided for mentees and mentors. As it was with my sushi progression, going outside of your comfort zone in attempting instructional practices when another teacher or coach is guiding you along the way can result in satisfying experiences and feeling successful. Within Mentor Coaching Cycles, it allows instructional coaches an avenue to provide extra assistance and unique professional development experiences to both you and your new teacher. Mentors and mentees, in conjunction with an instructional coach, develop collective teacher efficacy and see the growth of double the students as a result. Celebrating this work is key, and the excitement promotes motivation for all cycle participants. The long-term effects from the original coaching experience can continue surfacing with both new teachers and mentors. This collaboration and positivity could then spread to other teachers and staff in the building.

MENTOR INQUIRY REFLECTION

Think back to your guiding questions at the beginning of the chapter. Take some time to reflect on the questions that follow as well as use the Rubric for Student-Centered Mentoring Section #6 to help set goals and make a plan for yourself (Figure 6.6).

1. How can you utilize the support of another colleague to help you and your mentee increase your student impact?

2. How can you incorporate components of Mentor Coaching Cycles in your mentoring partnership?

3. What connection can you make to the states of collective teacher efficacy that can be connected to student achievement growth?

4. Which Student-Centered Mentoring success criteria would you choose to support your mentoring partnership?

5. What are some initial action steps you can take to incorporate in-depth learning through coaching support?

Figure **6.6** **Rubric for Student-Centered Mentoring**

#6: Utilize the Additional Support of a Coach or Someone in a Similar Role		
Beginner	**Emerging**	**Innovative**
The mentor is unsure of what support to request from a coach or another colleague who may be able to support the mentee in a similar style.	The mentor is beginning to use the instructional coach for a resource and may be asking a coach for informal planning advice and/or doing an individual cycle with the mentee.	The mentor seeks instructional coaching to provide in-depth learning for the partnership that will encourage effective instructional practices and increase student learning.

Success Criteria

- I can help organize a Mentor Coaching Cycle with an instructional coach or someone in a similar role.

- I can participate in setting a student-centered goal and learning targets that will meet everyone's needs.

- I can use student work to encourage reflective planning and drive next steps.

- I can be flexible with co-teaching opportunities that balance shared support with my mentee.

- I can learn ways from the coach to give effective strengths-based feedback to my mentee, who can turnkey that approach with students.

- I can share the impact of coaching cycles on student and teacher learning.

APPENDIX A

Collection of Student-Centered Mentoring Questions and Language

Chapter 1
Questions to Consider for Signs of Struggling New Teachers • Are their beliefs affecting their practices in such a way that lowers their self-confidence? • Are they missing the passion of serving others? • Are the professional development sessions full of teacher-centered practices rather than a balance that includes more of a focus on student learning? • Is there a low level of collective efficacy or lack of collaborative culture within the school?
Mentor Role Clarification—Questions to Ask • Is there a mentor and/or mentee handbook? • Are stipends available? • Are extra planning periods possible? • Is substitute coverage available for meetings/observations? • Do other job responsibilities need to be adjusted? • How do you choose mentors?
Chapter 2
Reflective Student-Centered Questions for Mentors • What kind of questions are you asking your mentee in relation to the student outcomes? • Are you asking surface-level questions or going more in depth? • How are mentees themselves asking questions in relation to students? • What do the majority of your mentee's students experience when outside of school that could affect their day-to-day well-being?

(Continued)

Chapter 2
Student-Centered Planning Questions for Mentors
• What student work can we look at to guide next steps?
• How are the students showing you their learning?
• What do the majority of your students already know?
• How can we keep students engaged?
• Why do we want the students to learn this information?
• What instructional strategies match the students' needs at this time?
Discussion Guide for Listening
• What evidence can we use to be more intuitive with students?
◦ Student survey data
◦ Student achievement data
◦ Student observations
◦ Interviews or conversations
• How do we promote being better listeners with students?
◦ Class meeting discussions
◦ Book clubs
◦ Group work
◦ Partner reading
◦ Providing examples of listening characteristics
◦ Modeling being a listener during presentations
Chapter 3
Questions to Consider for Prioritizing Time
• How much time do we have for the lesson/activity?
• What are the high yield/high effect size instructional practices that will make the most of the allotted time?
• Will the times work for everything?
• What does the time look like? Sound like?
• Can I get everything done in that small amount of time?
• Do I have any time left?

Chapter 3

Discussion Questions to Promote Independent Learners

- What does learning look like?

- What does engagement look like? Sound like?

- How can all students be independent in their learning?

- How does the classroom environment support all students? Students with trauma? Students of different cultures? Students with learning difficulties?

- In what ways do our students in front of us learn?

- How do we get to know our students through our teaching?

Mentor Question Suggestions in Connection to the Ready for Rigor Framework

Awareness

- What are your brain's triggers around race and culture?

- What are some potential triggers that may be impeding your management of the classroom?

- How do I collect student evidence that ensures all students' participation?

Information Processing

- What are some cognitive routines that will signal learning shifts in the day?

- What are ideas for how I can connect content to students' community and everyday lives?

- How do I intentionally plan for equitable practices that reinforces the learning of all students?

Learning Partnerships

- What are some ways we can discuss our learning, beliefs, and experiences?

- What can we do to balance our time?

- How can we boost students' confidence and skills of working together?

Community of Learners and Learning Environment

- What are ideas for how I can connect content to students' community and everyday lives?

- What are some classroom rituals, specifically around how to share ideas?

- How can we be sure all students' voices are heard in our classroom?

(Continued)

(Continued)

Chapter 4
Questions to Promote Equitable Expectations
• What do we envision our low and high expectation of learning should be?
• How can we push learners to go higher than their own expectation?
• Are we equitable when it comes to our expectations of students?
• What do we expect the student outcomes to be?
• How do we think all students will perform?
Questions for Promoting a Student-Centered Classroom Set-Up
• What arrangement of desks/tables/seats can I have that promotes dialogue over monologue?
• Where do I set up my teacher areas and technology tools to best utilize instructional time (as well as save me time)?
• How can I promote a welcoming and collaborative environment for learning?
• What tools and resources need to have spaces to promote student independence?
• What charts and visuals need to be given priority and that also minimize student distractions?

Chapter 5
Questions to Promote Understanding of Instructional Strategies
• What does the strategy really mean?
• What is the purpose of the strategy?
• How does it look in the classroom?
Questions to Ask Students for Clarity of Learning (Almarode & Vandas, 2018)
• What are you learning?
• Why are you learning it?
• How will you know if you've learned it?

Chapter 6
Mentor Coaching Cycle Co-planning and Co-teaching Discussion Questions
• How will we co-teach together?
• Who will teach what part of a lesson/activity?
• What will the other teacher do when not teaching?
• What are some ways we can gather student evidence?
• How will we share our notes about students?

Chapter 6

The Seven Norms of Collaboration to Balance Mentor Coaching Cycle Conversations (Garmston & Wellman, 2016)

1. Pausing

2. Paraphrasing

3. Posing questions

4. Putting ideas on the table

5. Providing data

6. Paying attention to self and others

7. Presuming positive intentions

APPENDIX B

Learning Inquiry Activity

1. Have teachers answer and discuss questions about learning.

   What does learning look like in your mind?

   - Is learning sometimes hard?

   - Does learning have a problem?

   - Can you fail when you learn?

   - How do you feel about learning when asked to explain your reasoning, when you have to try something again, and when you don't understand?

   - Define a learning mindset.

2. Read the article, "Mindset to Believe."

3. Watch video, "You Can Learn Anything" https://www.youtube.com/watch?v=JC82Il2cjqA

4. Discuss definitions of a learning mindset.

5. Reflect on having a learning mindset using the Learning Mindset Progression.

6. Share reflections of the Learning Mindset Progression.

Learning Mindset Progression With Success Criteria

Fixed	Emerging	Growth	Innovator
The learner is accepting of the current level and will maintain skills and knowledge without question or risk-taking.	The learner is uncertain about attempting new skills and may work little by little to make small improvements.	The learner is inspired to increase achievement and is persistent in mastering new skills.	The learner is empowered to attempt to solve new problems and is passionate about improving critical thinking skills while being flexible with next steps.

Success Criteria

- I can set a focused goal and revise when needed.

- I can listen to feedback and take action in attainable steps.

- I can try out something new in manageable chunks.

- I can make time to ask questions and be creative.

- I can celebrate the easy and difficult steps in my practices.

APPENDIX C

Reflecting on the Year Handout

Part 1: What Can We Celebrate Thus Far for the Year?

What has gone well this year?

Part 2: Beliefs Reflection

What is a moment or experience that supported your passion for working with students this year?

Part 3: Goal-Setting for the Remainder of the Year

What are some of the listed ideas that stand out to you in the directional supports that would support you the remainder of the year? Brainstorm additional possibilities in an area you may want to focus on or more specific topics.

Emotional	Communication	Physical	Instructional
• Self-care routines • Student trauma • Social-emotional needs pertinent to age levels • Start a journal of moments • Family stressors and challenges	• Student recognition • Student behavior • Collaborating with colleagues • Parent-teacher conferences • Administrator evaluations	• Copier • Building drills • Room location • Staff meetings	• Methods • Engagement of students • Strategies and skills for students

What do you hope to accomplish for the remainder of the year as a partnership? Set a goal and make a three-step action plan for what you want to accomplish.

Goal

Action plan—next week, next month, and end of year

APPENDIX D

Needs Assessment on Expectations From Beliefs

Belief Statements	Based on My Current Group of Students or Situation, This Looks Like?
I believe all students have the ability to learn.	
I am confident I can motivate all students to learn.	
I am well prepared to teach the information I am assigned to teach.	
Learning takes place in my classroom because students are not worried about external factors in their home life.	
If a student in my classroom does not learn something the first time, we will try to find another way.	
It takes a collaborative effort to positively impact student learning.	
I am willing to try new methods to better meet the needs of my students.	
It is important to have conversations with colleagues about student learning.	
I like to observe other classrooms in order to grow my repertoire of instructional strategies.	
I will ask for feedback from another colleague, instructional coach, principal, or students.	
I have developed ways to cope when a stressful situation arises with students.	
I balance my time working with students and self-care throughout my day.	

REFERENCES

Almarode, J., & Vandas, K. L. (2018). *Clarity for learning: Five essential practices that empower students and teachers*. Corwin.

Bandura, A. (1986). *Social foundations of thought and action: A social cognitive theory*. Prentice-Hall.

Bandura, A. (1997). *Self-Efficacy: The exercise of control*. W. H. Freeman.

Boogren, T. (2015). *Supporting beginning teachers*. Marzano Research.

Brown, B. (2012). *Daring greatly: How the courage to be vulnerable transforms the way we live, love, parent, and lead*. Penguin Group.

Brueggeman, A. C. (2018). *Mentor and mentee collective efficacy, professional development, and coaching cycle effects on literacy achievement* [Unpublished doctoral dissertation]. Maryville University.

Carrington, J. (2019). *Kids these days: A game plan for (re)connecting with those we teach, lead, & love*. FriesenPress.

Casey, J., & Costas-Bissell, C. (2021, July 21-22). *Leveraging student voice to know, act, and evaluate our impact* [Conference presentation]. Virtual Annual Visible Learning Conference.

Cherry, K. (2020). What is negativity bias? Retrieved July 9, 2021, from https://www.verywellmind.com/negative-bias-4589618

Couros, G. (2014, December 1). 8 characteristics of the "Innovator's Mindset." Retrieved August 23, 2020, from https://connectedprincipals.com/archives/11040

Couros, G. (2015). *The innovator's mindset: Empower learning, unleash talent, and lead a culture of creativity*. Dave Burgess Consulting.

Donohoo, J. (2013). *Collaborative inquiry for educators: A facilitator's guide to school improvement*. Corwin.

Donohoo, J. (2017). *Collective efficacy: How educators' beliefs impact student learning*. Corwin.

Duckworth, A. (2016). *Grit: The power of passion and perseverance*. Scribner.

Dweck, C. (2016). *Mindset the new psychology of success*. Random House.

Ferguson, K. (2014). How three schools view the success of literacy coaching: Teachers', principals' and literacy coaches' perceived indicators of success. *Reading Horizons, 53*(1), 1-37. https://www.ebscohost.com

Fisher, D., Frey, N., Amador, O., & Assof, J. (2019). *The teacher clarity playbook: A hands-on guide to creating learning intentions and success criteria for organized, effective instruction*. Corwin.

Foltos, L. (2013). *Peer coaching: Unlocking the power of collaboration* (77-99). Corwin. https://www.ebscohost.com

Garmston, R. J., & Wellman, B. M. (2016). *The adaptive school: A sourcebook for developing collaborative groups*. Rowman and Littlefield.

Gay, G. (2010). *Culturally responsive teaching theory, research, and practice*. Teachers College Press, Teachers College, Columbia University.

Goddard, R., Hoy, W., & Woolfolk Hoy, A. (2000). Collective teacher efficacy: Its meaning, measure, and impact on student achievement. *American Educational Research Journal, 37*(2), 479-507.

Goddard, R., Hoy, W., & Woolfolk Hoy, A. (2004). Collective efficacy beliefs: Theoretical developments, empirical evidence, and future directions. *American Educational Research Association, 33*(3), 3-13.

Goodreads. (2021). Xun Kuang quote. https://www.goodreads.com/quotes/7565817-tell-me-and-i-forget-teach-me-and-i-may

Hammond, Z. (2015). *Culturally responsive teaching and the brain: Promoting authentic engagement and rigor among culturally and linguistically diverse students.* Corwin.

Hattie, J. (2012). *Visible learning for teachers: Maximizing impact on learning.* Routledge.

Hattie, J. (Producer). (2020). *The power of feedback.* [Webinar] hosted by GrokSpot & NextLesson.

Hattie, J., & Zierer, K. (2018). *10 mindframes for visible learning: Teaching for success.* Routledge.

Hollie, S. (2013). *Culturally and linguistically responsive teaching and learning: Classroom practices for student success.* Shell Education.

Khan Academy. (2014, August 19). *You can learn anything.* Retrieved December 30, 2020, from https://www.youtube.com/watch?v=JC82Il2cjqA

KickUp Study. (n.d.). *The impact of student-centered coaching.* https://dianesweeney.com/wp-content/uploads/2018/07/The-Impact-of-Student-Centered-Coaching.pdf

Ladson-Billings, G. (2009). *The dreamkeepers: Successful teachers of African American children.* Jossey-Bass.

Marzano, R. J., & Simms, J. A. (2013). *Coaching classroom instruction.* Marzano Research Laboratory.

McCoach, D., & Colbert, R. (2010). Factors underlying the collective teacher efficacy scale and their mediating role in the effect of socioeconomic status on academic achievement at the school level. *Measurement and Evaluation in Counseling and Development, 43*(1), 31-47. https://doi.org/10.1177/0748175610362368

Miller, S., & Stewart, A. (2013). Literacy learning through team coaching. *The Reading Teacher, 67*(4), 290-298. https://doi.org/10.1002/TRTR.1219

Minero, E. (2017). *When students are traumatized, teachers are too.* https://www.edutopia.org/article/when-students-are-traumatized-teachers-are-too

Minor, C. (2019). *We got this: Equity, access, and the quest to be who our students need us to be.* Heinemann.

Nowik, O. (2015, July 27). *These 10 things would happen when you start stepping out of your comfort zone.* Retrieved December 18, 2020, from https://www.lifehack.org/291049/these-10-things-will-happen-when-you-start-stepping-out-you-comfort-zone

Oxford Dictionary. (2021). *Expectation.* Retrieved January 24, 2021, from https://www.lexico.com/en/definition/expectation

Stone, D., & Heen, S. (2014). *Thanks for the feedback: The science and art of receiving feedback well.* Penguin Group.

Sweeney, D. (2011). *Student-centered coaching: A guide for K-8 coaches and principals.* Corwin.

Sweeney, D. (2015). Not all pressure is positive pressure. *Diane Sweeney Consulting.* https://dianesweeney.com/not-pressure-positive-pressure/

Sweeney, D. & Harris, L. (2017). *Student-centered coaching: The moves.* Corwin.

Sweeney, D., & Harris, L. (2020). *The essential guide to student-centered coaching: What every K-12 coach and school leader needs to know.* Corwin.

Tschannen-Moran, M., & Barr, M. (2004). Fostering student learning: The relationship of collective teacher efficacy and student achievement. *Leadership and Policy in Schools, 3*(3), 189-209. https://doi.org/10.1080/15700760490503706

Visible Learning MetaX. (n.d.a). Retrieved September 21, 2020, from https://www.visiblelearningmetax.com/influences/view/classroom_discussion

Visible Learning MetaX. (n.d.b). Retrieved December 30, 2020, from https://www.visiblelearningmetax.com/influences/view/collective_teacher_efficacy

Visible Learning MetaX. (n.d.c). Retrieved January 5, 2021, from https://www.visiblelearningmetax.com/influences/view/teacher_estimates_of_achievement_

Visible Learning MetaX. (n.d.d). Retrieved January 30, 2021, from https://www.visiblelearningmetax.com/influences/view/teacher_clarity

Visible Learning MetaX. (n.d.e). Retrieved Jan 5, 2021 from https://www.visiblelearningmetax.com/influences/view/parental_expectations

Waack, S. (2021). *Glossary of Hattie's influences on student achievement*. Retrieved January 11, 2021, from https://visible-learning.org/glossary/

INDEX

Confident Teachers,
Inspired Learners

**CARLA MARSCHALL,
ELIZABETH O. CRAWFORD**

Nurture "Worldwise Learners": students who both deeply understand and purposefully act when learning about global challenges.

**JULIE STERN, KRISTA FERRARO,
KAYLA DUNCAN, TREVOR ALEO**

Harness the critical concepts of traditional disciplines while building students' capacity to transfer their learning to solve novel and complex modern problems.

CHASE NORDENGREN

Demonstrate goal setting as an integral instructional strategy to help students take ownership of their learning.

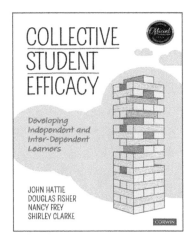

**JOHN HATTIE, DOUGLAS FISHER,
NANCY FREY, SHIRLEY CLARKE**

Working with other people can be a powerful accelerator of student learning and a precursor to future success.

To order your copies, visit **corwin.com/teachingessentials**

No matter where you are in your professional journey, Corwin aims to ease the many demands teachers face on a daily basis with accessible strategies that benefit ALL learners.

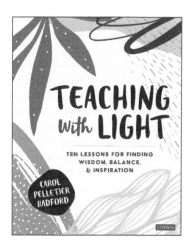

CAROL PELLETIER RADFORD

Equip teachers with the tools they need to take care of themselves so they can serve their students, step into leadership, and contribute to the education profession.

STEPAN MEKHITARIAN

Combine the best of distance learning and classroom instruction with a new vision for learning and professional development that capitalizes on the distance learning experience.

SERENA PARISER, VICTORIA S. LENTFER

Find actionable answers to your most pressing questions on how to create and sustain dynamic classroom.

STEPHANIE SMITH BUDHAI, KRISTINE S. LEWIS GRANT

Help teachers pivot instruction to ensure equitable, inclusive learning experiences in online and in-person settings.

CORWIN

A SAGE Publishing Company

Helping educators make the greatest impact

CORWIN HAS ONE MISSION: to enhance education through intentional professional learning.

We build long-term relationships with our authors, educators, clients, and associations who partner with us to develop and continuously improve the best evidence-based practices that establish and support lifelong learning.